WHAT CUSTOMERS
REALLY
WANT

How to Bridge the Gap Between What Your Organization
Offers and What Your Clients Crave

Scott McKain

THOMAS NELSON
Since 1798

NASHVILLE DALLAS MEXICO CITY RIO DE JANEIRO BEIJING

This book is dedicated to the bravest person I know—my wife, Sheri. Throughout your battle with the challenge of cancer, you have maintained an unbreakable spirit and a remarkable determination. To say that I love you seems so small compared to the pride I feel to have shared so many wonderful experiences with you. You are my hero.

After the writing and hardcover release of this book, my wife, Sheri, concluded her battle with cancer and departed for eternity in Heaven in June 2005. God richly blessed me by bringing her into my life—and I am so grateful for the quarter-century we had together.

Copyright © 2005 by Scott McKain

Published in Nashville, Tennessee, by Thomas Nelson, Inc.

Nelson books may be purchased in bulk for educational, business, fundraising, or sales promotional use. For information, please email SpecialMarkets@ThomasNelson.com.

Library of Congress Cataloging-in-Publication Data

McKain, Scott.
    What customers really want : bridging the gap between what your organization offers and what your customers crave / Scott McKain.
        p. cm.
    Includes bibliographical references.
    ISBN-13: 978-0-7852-1198-3 (hardcover)
    ISBN-10: 0-7852-1198-5 (hardcover)
    ISBN-13: 978-0-7852-8836-7 (trade paper)
    ISBN-10: 0-7852-8836-8 (trade paper)
    1. Relationship marketing. 2. Marketing—Psychological aspects. 3. Consumer behavior. 4. Customer services—Management. 5. Customer relations—Management. 6. Organizational effectiveness. I. Title.
HF5415.55.M34 2005
658.8'12—dc22   2004025625

Printed in the United States of America

07 08 09 10 RRD 7 6 5

CONTENTS

THE FUNDAMENTAL DISCONNECT

"What's the Difference?"

When your customers determine where they want to do business, do they look at you and your competition and ask themselves, "What does it matter? What's the difference between one and the other?" It doesn't matter what *your* answer is—if *they* don't notice and understand the difference, there is none.

I've always been a fan of the movies—probably no surprise to read from an author who previously wrote a book titled *ALL Business Is Show Business*! Because of my passion for the cinema, I was invited several years ago to offer my film reviews on a local television station. The reviews became so popular that I was eventually syndicated to eighty TV stations across America and three other countries. When I was a movie critic, I very seldom gave a motion picture all five stars—a perfect score. Thus, I was often asked what qualified a movie to be rated as a "five-star film."

My answer was simple—there were two basic tests. For the first test, I would ask myself, "Did *you* [not the audience in general, but me *specifically*] care passionately about the characters and what happened to them? Were you so caught up in what was happening to the characters that you were emotionally impacted by the events of the film?" My belief is if you become engaged to the point that you feel you know the people on the screen and they matter emotionally to you, the movie has passed the first "five-star test."

The second test, however, is the more difficult. "After you left the theater, were you so moved and connected—regardless if it was by laughter or romance or sorrow—that the first thing you had to do was tell a buddy about the movie? Were you so thrilled by the experience that you couldn't wait to recommend it—even to the point of telling a friend if he didn't love it as much as you did, you would buy his ticket?" If the film passes *both* tests—and the second test will never happen unless the first is answered in the affirmative—then a movie deserves the five-star ranking.

So, how would your *business do on the five-star test?*

What are your customers feeling and saying about you? Because if they are feeling disconnected—if they are not emotionally engaged in your "production"—and if they aren't saying anything to the people or organizations they influence, you are in serious trouble.

Looking Around at Starbucks

I was sitting in my local Starbucks, staring at my laptop and wondering how to begin this book. As I looked around, I noticed my fellow customers—students cramming, moms taking a short break, professionals such as myself getting a little work done outside the office on a wireless high-speed Internet connection, and couples on their way to or from a day of golf—and it struck me.

Right now, I am a customer at a coffee shop. So I came here to get a cup of coffee, right? Well, yes and no. I certainly have the coffee I purchased sitting next to me—however, what I *really* wanted was that *and much more.*

And that's what this book is about—what your customers REALLY want. The goal of this book is to show you how you can be certain that your organization is bridging the gap between what you offer and what your customers crave.

Sure, the Starbucks example has been used way too often—but for good reason. They "get it" in a way most organizations do not. They understand that what their customers crave isn't just coffee. And that is the great lesson all organizations need to understand.

So, Here's What Customers REALLY Want!

What do customers REALLY want? Ready? Here it is: Customers desire a *connection* with the people and organizations with whom they do business so the outcome is a compelling experience that transcends mere transactions.

They want to feel as if you care for them as much as they cared for a character in a five-star film. They want to believe that you worry as much about *them* as you do their business. And they want to do business with an organization they can advocate and recommend to their friends with as much passion as they do a five-star film.

Customers want a *connection* that transcends mere transactions.

The deeper the connection, the deeper the loyalty. The more tenuous the connection, the more the customer is looking for someplace else to do business.

In his terrific book *Purple Cow,* Seth Godin says that your business must become "remarkable." I agree—and want to take it a step further: your product or service must become *compelling*.

You may have a remarkable product or service; however, if you cannot provide a compelling reason for a customer to do business with you, you do not deserve a dime of the customer's money. Here is a question that I want you to consider carefully before answering: What is compelling about doing business with you and your organization? If you cannot answer that—and answer with a degree of passion—you probably don't have that type of powerful connection with your customer.

The problem is, many of us are working without a compelling product. Sure, you would love for your company to have the next iPod coming out of R & D. In the real world, you may not be able to go out and create the next extraordinary product or service; therefore, you'll have to find a way to make something else about your business compelling for customers. That aspect could be the connection you establish—the relationship you maintain—with your clients.

The Disconnect in American Business

So why do most businesses fail in this regard?

As I have researched the problem—not only for this book and my speeches, but for the organizations I own and assist in managing—I have discovered *six major areas* in which there is a tremendous and surprising disconnection between businesses and the customers they seek to serve. My position is that this gap is driving the extraordinary degree of dissatisfaction that many customers and clients have with the providers of their goods and services.

Remember Howard Beale?

If you are over forty—or a movie fan—you undoubtedly remember Howard Beale, the beleaguered television anchor played by the late Peter Finch in the Oscar-winning movie *Network*. His famous line was "I'm as mad as hell, and I'm not going to take it anymore!"

That line had significant resonance when the film was first released in 1976. The scary thing is that, for many businesses, the phrase is now a cliché that has minimal impact because, in one way or another, customers and clients are expressing it in varied ways *every single day* to organizations that cannot—or will not—deliver to them what they REALLY want.

My experience as vice chairman of the publicly traded Obsidian Enterprises and its sister organization, the privately held Durham Capital Corporation, and from speaking to the world's leading organizations on client relationships, is that there is simply a stunning disconnect between what customers seek and what organizations deliver.

I believe this is the single most critical element for business success and growth in the twenty-first century. I know this is true—not only because I've researched it diligently and constantly discussed it at large conventions and in small, private workshops—but also because my partners and I have built one of the fastest-growing companies in America by using our innovative philosophy. That's why the goal of this book is to provide candid, straight talk that is basic, yet insightful. Fancy philosophies won't get the job done for your customers without specific, proven strategies that you can execute.

The Goal That Makes a Difference . . .

Your goal should be to provide what customers REALLY want so you can generate increasingly higher levels of consumer loyalty. Unlike "customer satisfaction surveys," which measure what customers *say* they think (not how they actually behave), customer loyalty measurement provides you the hard numbers concerning the way they *act and spend.*

Do you and your organization even measure customer commitment and retention? Do you have a strategy to create enhanced customer loyalty?

According to Frederick Reichheld in his book *The Loyalty Effect*— using the banking industry as an example—if a bank will increase customer retention by just 5 percent, it will result in an *85 percent aggregate increase in the net present value* of an institution's branch deposits!

Let's take the total field of financial services as just one example: in that industry it costs $280 for a retail financial service firm, on average, to find a new customer. The average cost of keeping a customer is only *$57*, according to a Gartner survey released by the company on August 8, 2002, and found on their corporate Web site. Yet so many organizations spend an incredible amount of time and effort to get new customers in the front door—never realizing that they would be better off to keep the current customers from fleeing out the back door.

A report by the *Las Vegas Review-Journal* covering the 2003 convention of the National Grocers Association said it well: "Community-based retailers must develop a strong brand identity and offer unique products and services to differentiate themselves from 'big-box' retailers," the article begins. "'It all comes down to consumer choice, and the operative word there is 'choice,' said Ryan Mathews, executive editor of Grocery Headquarters Magazine.'"[1]

Mr. Mathews is exactly right. Now more than ever, your customers have a wider array of options from which to choose. But what if all those options have a similar look and feel?

"If everything is the same, there is no choice," Mathews said during a convention general session, according to the February 4, 2003, article. "The future lies in offering a clear alternative that has value. This industry [grocery stores and supermarkets], like so many American industries, is focusing on the symptoms and not the disease."

> Business owners like to blame consumers for not being loyal, but in many cases, they haven't given their customers any reason to be loyal.

The news article continues: "Mathews said business owners like to blame consumers for not being loyal, but in many cases, they haven't given their customers any reason to be loyal. They're too focused on advertising item and price because that's how they've done it for 80 or 90 years."

Don't I know that! My father and mother had the stereotypical mom-and-pop grocery store in my hometown of Crothersville, Indiana. I grew up learning the value of customer connections by watching my father, who was one of the best I've ever seen at cultivating relationships with his customers. That relationship building was the major factor that enabled our little store to survive the onslaught of the "big-box" retailer that has doomed so many other, less-focused businesses. The "big box" didn't succeed in our town, but not because my family's store advertised a cheaper price for Tide. It was because they couldn't compete with my father in the area of relationship cultivation.

"Things have changed," Mathews continues in the *Review-Journal* article. "Ozzie Nelson has been replaced with Ozzy Osbourne. What we need to do is think about the permanent change in the way people shop."

If for no other reason—forgetting that it's just the *right* thing to do—providing what customers REALLY want is *smart* and *profitable.*

Organizations Must Learn What Their Customers REALLY Want

Think about it: neither Tiger Woods, Vijay Singh, nor Phil Mickelson begins a golf tournament merely hoping to make the cut. They all focus on the ultimate position—first place. Yet, supposedly smart companies will develop strategies to improve their customer satisfaction survey scores by a mere 0.3 percent. And when they achieve that very modest goal, they then presume their customers are satisfied and that satisfaction will ensure their loyalty.

The companies cited most frequently as the amazing examples of customer experiences—to the point that they have now become corporate clichés, just like Howard Beale's cinematic citation—did not begin by targeting tiny, incremental improvements. The key is to shoot for a *total* customer connection by knowing what your clients *really* want from you. You've heard some of the stories before: Disney theme parks differentiate through the experience. So do Southwest Airlines, Nordstrom, and, of course, Starbucks. However, I believe much of what is discussed about these companies misses the mark in terms of providing insight to their amazing success. And there are many examples from smaller, relatively unknown companies (for example, one of our subsidiaries, Pyramid Coach) that are differentiating themselves in the marketplace by understanding how to fight customer disconnection.

Do Customers Trust You and Your Organization?

Yet another problem that organizations face in dealing with customers is the lack of faith and trust their clients may have because of negative experiences they have endured at other businesses. In an article titled "The Tyranny and Opportunity of the Customer Disconnect" (ABA *Bank Marketing* magazine, October 2002), Robert Hall of Carreker Corporation wrote, "Every time a major company creates distrust through its actions with customers, it erodes the level of trust that customers have with *all* of their providers." In other words, just as the scars of a difficult previous relationship may taint your ability to create new romantic involvements, when one company damages a relationship with a client, that same customer will then bring baggage into his or her relationship with you.

Hall continued, "When customers perceive they live in a world where the motives of providers cannot be trusted, they ardently seek trustful relationships. It's more than a desire to avoid getting 'taken'— more than a wish to avoid dealing with sleazy people. In a world where time has become such a premium, distrust is just so inefficient."

That's a great line: *distrust is just so inefficient.* If for no other reason than to enhance the efficiency of your organization, now is the time to develop and execute the strategies that provide your customers with what they *really* want.

The Corporate Vaccine

One more point on this—what happens if things go wrong for your company? What happens if there is a problem that creates a challenge for your organization? None of us enjoys considering this—yet there are so many examples that come to mind. In their study "Toward Understanding the Value of a Loyal Customer," University of Kansas professor Rohini Ahluwalia and Ohio State's Rao Unnava and Robert Burnkrant determined that brand commitment pays returns for a business at the time the business needs it most.

In the study, they examined the problem Chrysler faced when the rear-door locks were found to be faulty on its minivans. Those who were not loyal customers found that a fault with locks impacted their perceptions about *all other* aspects of the minivan. These potential customers questioned whether other features of the car were reliable. In other words, they were saying, "If the locks are faulty—what else about the car is going to be trouble?"

Those who were already loyal Chrysler customers would respond to the problem by saying, according to Ahluwalia, "I understand the lock

THE FUNDAMENTAL DISCONNECT

is faulty, but they're replacing it. It's *just* the lock." In other words, if you are already loyal to the company and the brand, you will be inclined to continue to think *positively* about it—even during problematic situations—and you're less likely to switch to a competitor.[2]

In writing about this study in the newsletter *Insights* from Marketing Science Institute, Mary B. Young said, "Like a preventative drug, it [customer loyalty] builds resistance to future illness."

So . . . what is the basis of customer loyalty? It's not "just" customer service. It is knowing and then providing what customers REALLY want—and understanding that executing this strategy is like a vaccine for your organization.

The Business Lesson of Lance Armstrong

Tour de France winner and cancer survivor Lance Armstrong is the author of the inspirational best seller *It's Not About the Bike* (Penguin Putnam, 2000). While there's no doubt that Mr. Armstrong has been very successful in writing one of the most touching and motivational books to come along in quite a while, he would probably be a bit surprised to learn that it could be considered as a text with great insight into business.

It's *not* about the bike—it *is* about the person riding it. It's *not* about your product—it *is* about the people who use it, build it, sell it, and manage it. Your challenge is to find out the specifics about what the people who buy and use your products and services REALLY want so you can enhance the total experience they have in dealing with your organization.

Starting My Business . . .

A few years ago, my best friend, Tim Durham, said to me, "Scott, I love your ideas about customer relationships. Let's go buy a company and put them into practice." My first reaction was—in all honesty— "You gotta be kidding! With my *own* money?" (It is infinitely easier to tell other people how they should be running their business than it is to manage your own!)

However, my second reaction was that if there is anyone in the world I would want to be in business with, it's Tim Durham. Here's a guy who graduated in the top percentile of his undergraduate class with a degree in mathematics (making my BA in political science pale by comparison), and then went on to graduate in the top three of his law school class. Tim literally has the most brilliant business mind of anyone I have ever encountered. He reads a balance sheet the way Peyton Manning reads a defense. It is amazing to watch as he quickly evaluates a business and often discovers points—with what appears to be merely a cursory glance—that many "experts" failed to catch in a detailed analysis. He's so good, it's scary.

What Tim was really saying to me was that we should combine his ultrahigh level of business finance acumen with my viewpoint about customer relationships to build a business. I knew I *had* to be part of that!

Obsidian Enterprises is a company I will refer to often in this book—in part because of a bias I will readily admit. I've read way too many business books written by people who have absolutely zero frontline experience. It is my goal to be certain you understand that the concepts and ideas I present about customer relationships and service are not just theory—instead they are strategies that you can practice in your organization . . . just as we have practiced them in our own.

Our Bus Company: Pyramid Coach

One of the companies we have acquired is Pyramid Coach, based near Nashville, Tennessee. Pyramid was already a moderately successful company, transporting country music stars across the nation to their concerts. Our vision was that we could take Pyramid to the next level, and become one of the primary players in the celebrity coach business.

It is no coincidence that the first detailed story I'm telling you in this book is an example of a time we almost failed our customers. We learn best from our errors! We at Obsidian congratulated one another on being in the "bus business." Big mistake.

Immediately we began to consult with interior decorators and the craftspersons who could build and install the designers' new and breathtaking ideas for upgrading the insides of these very expensive coaches. Our thinking was pretty obvious—if you enhance the interior of the bus, then you should be able to charge your customers a higher rate for the lease of the vehicle and make more money. We had gone through the process of picking out fabric, flooring, and all the accoutrements when the "blinding flash of the obvious" hit us—was this approach what our customers REALLY wanted?

In all honesty, it had never occurred to us to even ask. Surely if they were leasing a bus, they would want the best bus they could get at a reasonable lease price—wouldn't they? That should be obvious, we assumed.

And, as is often the case, unfounded assumptions can be very off target.

The Critical Question

During a discussion regarding Pyramid, I suggested to Tim; our chief operating officer, Terry Whitesell; and the vice president of finance, Jeff Osler, that if our coach company were a *client* of mine, I would first ask if they had surveyed their customers to find out what *they* really wanted. We had not yet done that—and we realized that we must get started.

In all fairness, I also insisted that I believed we were already on the right track—better interiors and better buses meant a higher level of client and, therefore (I assumed), more revenue from the lease of the coach.

Here's the way the celebrity coach business works: Leading entertainers, for example in country music, lease or purchase these incredible custom-designed buses to take the star and his or her band and road crew to play at their numerous concerts. Coach companies, like ours, will purchase a bus "shell" from one of the major manufacturers—in our case, mostly from the Canadian company Prevost. The shell looks exactly like what the name implies—imagine the interior basically being little more than a steering wheel and pedals at the front. After we take delivery of that shell, we begin to do a "conversion."

That's the term used in the industry to describe the design, manufacture, and installation of the extraordinary interiors you may have seen on various entertainment television shows. (For example, if you've ever seen Ozzy Osbourne on his bus on the MTV show *The Osbournes*, you've seen a Pyramid coach. Ozzy and Sharon Osbourne are two of our biggest fans and best customers. A little more on that later . . .)

Conversion design happens in two ways: One, a celebrity or band will assist in managing the design so that the interior is fitted to the individual's or group's specific and personal needs and tastes. When this happens, the act is signing a longer-term lease or purchasing the bus outright, since the coach is created to those specifications.

Or, two, we work with a decorator to create the interior in a style we find appealing—and somewhat generic—so that multiple acts will lease the coach for shorter periods of time. As an example, the enduring band Chicago may tour for six months in our coaches, then take the rest of the year to record and relax. Another act—perhaps country superstar Alan Jackson—will then book the same bus for the next six months for his concert tour.

Frankly, in most situations, we prefer our clients to lease (rather than purchase) a bus from us. With purchase, the client might choose to use us to service the coach, or may try to get it done elsewhere. Because the active use of the coach is for many years—and because an individual performer probably will not purchase many coaches in his or her career—a sale reduces the opportunity for a longer-term relationship.

And, just as you find with automobile manufacturers who provide customer financing, there's more money in a lease than in a sale. Most significant, however, is that when a band like Chicago leases a coach, a relationship with ongoing contact has begun. On a lease, we're always there to service the bus, schedule the trips, and, most important, provide and supervise the driver.

Pyramid has many worthy competitors, particularly in the Nashville market. That's why we wanted to ensure that when a star or manager looked at our bus, that person would be knocked out by the accommodations he or she would be enjoying during the long hours spent traveling to and from concerts.

However, we realized that it was important to provide what our customers REALLY wanted—and the only way we would know for certain was to *ask* them. So, we did.

The Surprising Result

Imagine our astonishment when we asked clients like country superstars Alan Jackson and Brad Paisley, pop group Chicago and Ozzy and Sharon Osbourne (well . . . we couldn't really understand Ozzy's answer, so we asked Sharon!)—only to discover that, while they did want well-appointed interiors, an overriding concern when selecting the company with whom they would do business was better bus *drivers*!

Picture yourself waking up in your bunk in the bus at 3:00 AM. Do you really want to lie there and worry if the driver is a safe operator?

Imagine the varied—and sometimes outrageous—personalities found in a touring musical group. Obviously, the driver needs to fit in, yet not get too involved with the everyday problems of the group. He or she must be able to get along with many personality types and overlook many idiosyncrasies. The driver becomes both confidant(e) and counselor—while at the same time holding him- or herself to the ultimate standards of behavior and professionalism.

Pretend that you are a huge fan of the hot alternative rock band Staind. You arrive early at the show, hoping to get a glimpse of your favorite group. You notice the driver standing by the bus and strike up a small conversation. It would never occur to you that the driver is a Pyramid employee—you would naturally presume the driver works for Staind. Drivers—whether for new rock acts or established country stars—are ambassadors of that act to the fans.

Yet we were focusing solely on the bus. Our customers could obtain the use of a coach from us—*or* from our competitors. Most of us were using identical Prevost coaches for the shell. And there are many terrific designers and conversion manufacturers out there, all capable of creating incredible interiors for their clients. We realized that the sole factor of differentiation—unless we just wanted to play a lowball, cut-the-price-to-the-bone, think-only-of-the-short-term strategy—was the *driver*.

We immediately began a driver education program.

The Role of Education in Your Efforts

It's my *strong* belief that you should *not* have a "training department" or "training programs." Don't get me wrong—I believe every organization should invest in the development and growth of its people. My problem is with the word *training*.

You bring a puppy home for the first time—and what's one of the first things you do? You start to *train* the dog to "go on the paper." Then you move your *training* outdoors, so the dog will "go outside." You devise various strategies to *train* the little puppy where to pee. And, heaven forbid, when the little dog has an "accident," not only is he usually scolded, but we *rub his nose on the wet spot to reinforce our training*!

The next morning, this same person who is trying to get her dog to "go to the bathroom" in the proper place arrives at work, where she's informed that she is now going to take part in corporate *training*! What's her gut-level, visceral reaction to "training" at this point? You train a puppy—you *educate* your people! (And, I should point out the implication that if she messes up, her nose will get rubbed in her mistake, too!)

You train a
puppy—you
educate your
people!

So we started educating the drivers of Pyramid. They learned how to communicate more effectively with varied personality types, how to resolve conflicts, and how to think in terms of retaining and growing customer relationships. We also changed the reward system so that drivers were compensated not only for how many miles they had driven, but also for how completely they were serving the customer. They were given bonuses for creating long-term relationships—and for turning mere transactions into a differentiated experience for the people riding their buses.

The Real Lesson for (and from) Pyramid

Here's what we really learned from this process: to paraphrase Lance Armstrong, "It's not about the bus. It *is* about the people inside it." Those people are your customers and employees.

Again, in most cases your customers can obtain a relatively similar product or service from one of your rivals. We know our customers can certainly find great celebrity coaches from competitors such as Hemphill and Music City Coach, among others. Until you understand that "it's not about the bus," you'll never be motivated to find out what customers REALLY want.

My guess is that anyone who spends time really focusing on corporate endeavors will at some point have to develop his or her own unique slant on the purpose of business. This exercise should not be some lame attempt to contribute to the lexicon of corporate America, but to develop a personal and specific take on the nature of the beast called business. You and I have heard many philosophies, including "The purpose of business is to make a profit," or "The purpose of business is to obtain and retain customers profitably." Both are true, and both address our traditional thinking about the nature of business.

Yet, I think we can—and must—do better. Here's my take on the purpose of business, as stated in my book *ALL Business Is Show Business*:

> The purpose of any business is to profitably create experiences that are
> so compelling to customers that their loyalty is assured.

That means it's not about the bus. It's about viewing your business as the platform—the "stage," if you will—from which you present what the customer REALLY wants.

So . . . what's the end of the Pyramid story? Well, as it is with all businesses, that saga continues to be written on a day-to-day basis. We're only as good as our drivers make us today, tonight, and tomorrow. However, the results we have seen thus far are remarkable. We've grown from twenty-eight to fifty-six coaches. We have moved from fourth in the marketplace to, arguably, first place in terms of customer loyalty and profitability. We have drivers from the competition knocking on our doors and offering to come to work for us—and bring along the bands they are driving for our rivals. We have customers like the Osbournes, who are recommending us to their friends in the music industry—and even in some cases requesting that the opening acts for their shows use Pyramid for their transportation. We figure that when your customers are selling your product for you, you've done a pretty good job with your business, based on the purpose I cited.

Your business can do the same.

Before They Buy

What do customers want to see from your business before they decide to buy from you in the first place?

Klaus Hilgers and Jere Matlock, in their book *The Power of Agreement,* quote a survey that states the five steps to customer satisfaction. They are:

1. Reliability
2. Responsiveness
3. Assurance
4. Empathy
5. Tangibles

Let's briefly examine each of these steps:

Reliability

Perhaps at the top of the list of the worst things you can do is to fail to keep a promise to your customers. Later in this book, I'll describe how a company lost my loyalty after a decade of my being one of their best customers in the nation. Suffice it to say at this point that the fundamental reason was because I felt they had broken a promise.

Becoming a reliable provider is a difficult achievement for some organizations because it involves three distinct aspects. These are:

1. The reliability of your people

2. The reliability of your product

3. The reliability of your service and customer experience

All three must be acting in concert to establish your organization as a reliable provider of goods and services to your customers. Yet, many times organizations have a great product and people who just cannot deliver. Or they have superior people and product, yet they fail to do the basic "blocking and tackling"—such as getting billing correct or other specifics—that prevent them from creating reliable service experiences.

Verizon Wireless has made a major effort to make certain prospective customers know that a J. D. Power and Associates study, as well as one from the *Wall Street Journal*, lists it as "the most reliable choice for wireless customers." In fact, Verizon's entire advertising campaign has become a national catchphrase: "Can you hear me now? Good!" Why are these endeavors so important? Because we shop for reliable products.

Sprint fired out its own study—FCC records of "reportable service outages"—and found that Sprint was tops for the eighth straight year "with regard to service uptime." Why? Because being reliable is not just a tool for recruitment; it is a major factor in your ability to retain.

Product reliability is vitally important. That aspect—plus the four others that follow—create the impressions regarding the reliability of your people, your service, and how dynamically you create customer experiences.

Responsiveness

In my previous book, I mentioned a novel idea I had the time a mobile phone company hired me to speak: I would have them introduce me; then I would take out my personal phone (since I was already a customer of their company) and call 611 for customer service. Once someone came on the line to help me, I would begin my speech. I figured keeping the audience waiting for a few moments would really bring home the point of the importance of responsiveness.

Imagine my surprise when the company's representative shrieked, "Oh, you can't do that! We only have you booked to speak *for an hour*!"

Without a doubt, "responsiveness" is the first place they should begin to build enhanced consumer relationships.

Customer responsiveness involves all the "touches" a customer has with your company from the point at which he or she is only a prospect to well after the sale has been completed. It can be defined as "consistently providing the right solution in a timely fashion in a manner that holds value for your customer."

Assurance

If you want customers to stay, then you have to assure them:

- they have made the right decision in choosing to do business with you;
- you are going to be there to assist them if they have any difficulty; and
- you are going to hold your organization and its people accountable to ensure that the job gets done.

Assurance provides your customers with the confidence that everything is going to work out fine—and reinforces their acquisition decision. And, while reliability and responsiveness are the first steps, assurance is where you begin to enhance the relationship. Reliability and responsiveness can be products of your systems—assurance is a function of emotion. Customers have to *feel* assured, and emotions are the foundation of engagement and connection.

Empathy

"I feel your pain."

Whether he *really* did or not isn't the issue. A vast number of voters *believed* that Bill Clinton had a great deal of empathy for their challenges. They responded with their votes.

Does your customer believe that you truly empathize with him?

Very few products or services are sold because everything is perfect for the customer! Your clients seek to solve a problem, heal a hurt, enhance a business, have more fun, and make more money—any of a myriad of reasons. However, every one of those reasons requires that you *understand and empathize* with their situations.

Tangibles

My good friend, noted author, speaker, and new president of High Point University, Nido Qubein, asks the professionals he consults if they have "left behind a trail of tangibles." In other words, after you have performed your service, is there something tangible . . . concrete . . . solid . . . that is left when you have departed?

It's a great question! Too often, we merely "do our jobs" or perform what we're "supposed" to do—and assume the customer will remember that we executed our tasks with professionalism. Ask yourself the important question, "Do WE leave behind a trail of tangibles, creating a compelling customer experience?"

Understand the Areas of Potential Disconnection

My research and practical experience have uncovered *six specific areas* of potential disconnection in a customer's experience. If you seek to provide what your customers REALLY want, these are the six points on which you should focus.

The disconnection happens because what business offers isn't always what customers are looking for. Yet, because most of us in business focus on "the bus," so to speak, we are oblivious to the disconnection.

Before we delineate the specific points of disconnection, ask this question of yourself and your organization: When did we last ask our customers what they REALLY want?

Focus on that for a moment—each word of the last part of that question has significance:

- *"what"*—specifically identify the "whats"—the aspects that would create a compelling difference for your organization with the customer.

- *"they"*—not *us* . . . them! An airline recently asked its customers if they would like low fares. As kids say today, "Well, *duh*!" Who wouldn't answer that in the affirmative? Yet, by asking the wrong question, the airline is getting the wrong answer. In other words, it asked customers a question for which management had already determined the answer. If you are going to provide what customers really want, you must approach them with an open mind!

- *"REALLY"*—In other words, in the real world. Sure, I would like it for free, have it delivered, and have you take care of all the details. However, we both know that is not going to happen. In the real world, there are several aspects that may be important to your customer that you haven't considered—or did not realize how important these points are. What customers REALLY want focuses on those aspects that will drive them to being loyal, committed buyers of your product or service.

- *"want"*—More than just a customer's wish or hope or basic need, this is asking customers to define their drivers for business. In many cases, organizations merely seek out the baseline. But if remarkable companies merely focused on the basics, rather than taking it to a higher level, there would be no need for Southwest to tell jokes and have fun on the flights . . . no need for Starbucks to do anything other than dish out coffee . . . no need for Nordstrom to have service any better than Kmart's . . . no need for Pyramid Coach to have drivers that respond to client needs. In other words, no need to *do the very things* that have made the business unique and successful.

The Six Customer Disconnections

So much could be written on how to establish more meaningful connections with customers; however, my opinion is that if we work to eliminate the disconnects, we remove the roadblocks and achieve the goal of our organizations: offering what our customers crave. As mentioned earlier, the purpose of this book is to help you discover the six essential disconnection points between organizations and the customers they

THE FUNDAMENTAL DISCONNECT

seek to serve. The disconnection is created by the variance between what clients are seeking and what business is serving.

Each of the following chapters will examine these six essential disconnection points. As you discover these points, it is vital that you examine your organization with an open mind and try to find how these issues relate to your specific situation. Your challenge is to create a meaningful, specific strategy that you can execute in your organization or department to make a significant difference—and provide significant differentiation—for your customers. Every chapter will outline how organizations (each of which occupies a prominent position within their niche market) have used these points to move from disconnection to powerful relationships and amazing customer loyalty.

Bridge Building

If you and your organization aspire to bridge the gaps and eliminate the disconnections between you and your customers, it's obvious that you're going to have to take action. Every chapter in this book will conclude with a short segment called "Bridge Building." Here, you will be able to start drawing up the plans for the steps you will take to reduce the gulf between your company and your clients.

My belief is that the best way for you to develop the action plan for execution is achieved through the posing of a series of questions. The optimum approach is to take a legal pad and just start jotting your answers to these queries. Then, ask the same questions of your colleagues and see if there are disconnections between their viewpoints and yours. Together you can develop the plans and build the bridges that will enable you to span the chasm between you and the clients and prospects you seek to serve.

o o o

It is possible for you to establish greater connections with your customers, provide them what they really want, *and* grow your business— all without expending significant amounts of money. *This is more of an exercise in commitment and execution than budget.* It's having the right philosophy about what your business is really all about.

I don't ask you to reexamine your business or department lightly—I'm well aware that this may be a provocative concept for many. When all of your efforts have tended to revolve around the product or service, to suggest that the very purpose of your business is to become compelling to your customer is heresy to some. This, in part, explains why the level of customer service often rises only to the height of lip service. In business we tend to be very insular. We listen to the same people internally, attend association meetings with other professionals from our same industry, and read the same trade journals as our competitors.

In the *Harvard Business Review* article of March 1, 2004, "The Geography of Trust," Saj-nicole Joni wrote, "Leaders who rely forever on the same internal advisers run the risk of being sold short and possibly betrayed." I believe the term *internal advisers* can mean not just those within your department or organization, but those within your specific industry as well. There is a great external source you can tap for information, insight, and innovation: *customers*. Tapping into their viewpoints is critical to building the connection that customers covet—and may provide the feedback you need to prevent the problem inherent in consistently listening to the same advice. Let's face it: though we hate to admit it, customers often know as much or more about our products or services than we do, because they are the ones using them in the real world.

They're "as mad as hell and not going to take it anymore"—and seeking a connection where they do business.

Here are the six points of customer disconnection:

What Customers REALLY Want	What Business Supplies
1. Compelling Experience	Customer Service
2. Personal Focus	Product Focus
3. Reciprocal Loyalty	Endless Prospecting
4. Differentiation	Sameness
5. Coordination	Confusion
6. Innovation	Status Quo

Let's begin with the first disconnection . . .

1

THE FIRST DISCONNECTION

What Customers REALLY Want: *Compelling Experience*
What Business Supplies: *Customer Service*

As I sat in the wrecked automobile, dust from the air bag covered my suit. My ears still ringing from the shotgunlike sound of the bag's deployment, I opened the car door and walked to the other driver to make certain he was OK.

I returned to my car and, finding my cell phone on the floorboard, I called the police. Then, still a little woozy from the accident, I realized there was another call I needed to make. I was driving a rental car from Hertz.

I pulled the car rental agreement from the glove compartment and found the number I knew was listed but had never had to use. The words on the folder read, "If you're in an accident, call the police and then call this number." I had called the police—now it was time to call Hertz and tell them I had just totaled one of their cars.

"This is Hertz," the kind voice on the other end of the line answered. "How may I help you?"

"Well, I hate to tell you this—I have never had to make one of these calls before—but I've just wrecked my rental car."

"Yes, sir—I understand. Are you all right?"

"Yes, ma'am, I'm fine. Thanks for asking."

"May I have your name, please?"

"Certainly . . . it's Scott McKain." My head was throbbing from the combination of the accident, the heat of the afternoon, and the stress of the traffic jam that had been caused (during rush hour in New York City!) by the accident. Suffice it to say that the middle-finger salutes our accident was eliciting were not out of concern for my health.

"Mr. McKain . . . are you absolutely sure that you are OK?" the Hertz representative inquired.

"Well—I am a little wobbly right now, but I'm not injured."

"I want to make certain," she said. "Hertz can always get another car—but we can *never* get another Mr. McKain."

That's when Hertz transcended from customer service to compelling experience—that's when they provided what I REALLY wanted.

Customer Satisfaction?

Let your imagination run free for a couple of minutes. Let's envision that you've met the person you believe to be your soul mate. She is absolutely perfect for you—the one with whom you want to spend the rest of your life. You send flowers and bring gifts. You wine and dine her with intensity and passion. On one knee and holding her hand, you nervously ask her how she feels about you and your new relationship. She responds, "Well . . . I guess I'm satisfied."

Are you thrilled with that answer? Of course not! You want her to be wildly, madly, crazy in love!

So, if "satisfaction" is such a disappointment to us in this situation, why do we find it so acceptable from our customers? Why don't we want them to be just as wildly, madly, crazily enthralled with our products and services? Why is mere "satisfaction" the supposed standard when it comes to our goals regarding clients?

In a June 2004 article titled "Beyond Mere Satisfaction, the Role of Customer Delight" by Timothy Keiningham, Douglas Pruden, and Terry Vavra, this amazing statistic is cited: "Over a five-year period of intense customer satisfaction activity (over $800,000,000 spent *annually* on customer satisfaction in the United States), the satisfaction ratings of American consumers have failed to increase!"[1]

One of their viewpoints states the obvious, but powerful, conclusion: "Surveying the results of this effort . . . one would have to conclude that far too few satisfaction programs have actually improved customers' satisfaction!"

Here are the statistics regarding what happens to dissatisfied customers and why they take their business elsewhere:

- Moved away from the area   3%
- Other friendships with providers   5%
- Chose the competition   9%
- Dissatisfaction with your product   14%
- Put off by an employee's attitude   68%

Other studies indicate that only 4 percent of dissatisfied customers will report their problem. Ninety-one percent of dissatisfied customers will never purchase anything from your company again (which, of course, speaks not only to the passion of dissatisfied customers, but also to the low quality of customer recovery efforts in place at most companies).

> Ninety-one percent of dissatisfied customers will never purchase anything from your company again.

Yet, is it possible that we have employed some pretty shaky logic in response to this research? What I mean is, after learning that customer dissatisfaction is so detrimental, we then make the seemingly logical assumption that what customers want must be "satisfaction." Makes sense, right? The opposite of "dissatisfaction" must be "satisfaction"—what else could it be?

Let's return to our example of romance discussed earlier—if the relationship proceeds in the manner you desire, the object of your affection will fall in love with you. However, what if the *opposite* occurs?

We tend to assume that the opposite of "love" is "hate." But if the woman you desire doesn't fall in love with you—does that mean she hates you? Of course not.

Psychologists will tell us that the opposite of love is not hate, because the emotion of hate still involves passion. The opposite of love is *indifference*.

The same is true with customer dissatisfaction. As strange as it sounds, the opposite of dissatisfaction is not satisfaction—because the research clearly shows that dissatisfied customers are staggeringly more passionate in their response than those that are merely "satisfied."

If satisfied customers responded in the inverse of dissatisfied customers, they would display a significant degree of loyalty, and that's just not the case.

My friend Jeffrey Gitomer authored a book with the classic title *Customer Satisfaction Is Worthless—Customer Loyalty Is Priceless.* I think that really says it all! Even those who claim to disagree with him have difficulty when they attempt to invalidate his point. In an article published November 2001 in *The Wise Marketer*, Michael Lowenstein calls Gitomer's phrase "both an exaggeration and a superficial reflection." Yet in practically the next breath he says, "Though there may be some tenuous relationship between satisfaction and loyalty (particularly in situations where there is little direct customer-supplier interaction), satisfaction metrics are generally very poor predictors of customer loyalty." Huh? Doesn't that statement help prove Gitomer's assertion?

Let me tell you how it is in our companies at Obsidian—we want loyal customers. If you're "satisfied" and still go somewhere else, that doesn't help us. So, to our companies, customer loyalty *is* priceless.

I believe part of the problem here is that we have three terms meaning different things, yet they are being used somewhat interchangeably:

1. customer satisfaction

2. customer service

3. customer experience

Until we understand that these three are very dissimilar, from the customer's point of view, it will be extraordinarily difficult to develop and execute the strategies necessary to create customer loyalty.

Experience or Service: What's the Difference?

As I give speeches across the country, I find that one of the most difficult concepts for professionals to grasp is the fundamental difference between customer *service* and the customer *experience*. To explain this, let's put the term *satisfaction* on the shelf for a bit and think of the three levels of customer interaction.

The Three Levels of Customer Interaction
Level One: Customer Processing

You have been there a million times—you're fourth in line at the drive-thru at a local fast-food restaurant. The line of cars moves slowly as they snake their way toward the speaker to place an order.

As you finally make it to the point where you can order your lunch, you are greeted with this sound from the speaker: "GOODAFTERNOONWELCOMETOBURGERKINGMAYI-TAKEYOURORDERPLEASE?"

The overmodulation from the speaker causes you to briefly recall a rock concert you attended in the early 1970s. (Why does it seem that technology has advanced everything but the speakers at drive-thrus?) You place your order for lunch and then hear, "THANKYOUNEXT-WINDOW."

A disinterested, gum-chewing cashier takes your money and points you to the next window, where an equally disinterested clerk pitches a bag of food at you. Have a nice lunch.

Sound familiar? Here's another:

You're waiting in a long line at the airport. When you finally arrive at the front, a ticket agent shouts, "NEXT!" You walk up and are greeted with these words: "Where's your destination today?" When you answer his question, he then responds with the ever-personal, "Name?"

He types your name and some mysterious code into the computer. He scrunches his mouth and waits, never looking at you. Evidently the computer screen has told the agent that you do, in fact, have a reservation—even an e-ticket for the flight—so the agent responds to his new information by saying, "Checking bags today?"

You check your bag, get your boarding pass, show your ID—and the agent never uses your name.

Now it's time for the thrilling portion of the trip we call "airport security." You stand in a long line to get to the point of screening—a line so enormous that it is putting you in danger of missing your plane. When you reach the front of the queue, you're told to strip off your belt, shoes, and dignity. You remove your laptop from your briefcase, spilling several items that you had carefully packed along the way. Thankfully, you didn't "beep"—and you can now make the mad dash so you won't miss your flight.

You arrive at the gate and the boarding process is like herding cattle at a slaughterhouse. The gate agent allows those with "special needs," children, elite-level fliers, passengers in first class, and those wearing yellow with the middle name "Sue" to board ahead of you. Then the people in the rear, then the middle . . . and by the time your group is announced, you are thanking God that you have no carry-on to attempt to place in the already-full overhead compartments.

You finally take your middle seat, stuffed between a retired sumo wrestler and the most recent parolee from your state's penitentiary—one row ahead of a mother with a crying baby and a four-year-old who won't stop kicking your seat. The frazzled flight attendants, who must serve a full plane in forty minutes, shovel you a lukewarm cup of coffee. After sixty minutes trapped in hell, you finally land at your destination.

In both cases, the business would—perhaps rightly—tell you it did its job. You were delivered a meal; you were delivered to your destination. You got your food, and you didn't have to wait an inordinate amount of time. You got where you wanted to go, had a cup of coffee, and arrived on time.

The problem is that there is a bad taste in your mouth . . . and it's not the fast food or airline coffee.

You weren't served as a customer—you were *processed*. That's Level One. Many organizations confuse "processing" with "service," creating a significant portion of the problems that customers have with the level of treatment they receive. In other words, because customers and companies define the very nature of customer service differently, many organizations miss the mark and fail to understand why.

Please don't misunderstand me—it is vital to improve the way your organization processes your customers' transactions. For example, take the case of the Speedpass payment system created by Mobil, now part of ExxonMobil. According to an article by Keith H. Hammonds in the November 2001 edition of *Fast Company* magazine:

Don't confuse processing with service.

> By waving a small device at a reader on the gas pump and having their credit cards automatically billed, customers could cut 30 seconds or so from a three-and-a-half-minute transaction. And that half-minute turned out to be compelling: Speedpass holders (5 million drivers have become active users in the past four years) average one visit more per month to Mobil stations than other customers do, and so spend 2% to 3% more per month. The company won't release conclusive data on Speedpass usage, but higher revenue so far has justified station owners' typical $15,000 investment in scanner technology.

By the way, note the word that *Fast Company* used to describe why Speedpass was important—it turned out to be *"compelling."*

Improving the speed and efficiency of a transaction is an improvement customers appreciate. However, this is also relatively simple for your competitors to duplicate. If you think just improving processing will give you a sustainable advantage in the marketplace, you are dead wrong. For example, another service station near my house is testing its own similar system.

Interestingly, ExxonMobil understood that point from the beginning. The *Fast Company* article continues, "Here's where Mobil has made a crucial leap in its thinking: The value of Speedpass isn't in the exclusivity of the technology. It's in the relationships with those 5 million users. That's a remarkably progressive analysis for the $230 billion leader of an industry known best for conservative, plodding strategy. Forfeit exclusivity, it says, in hopes of building something much more powerful." As the article clearly states, Speedpass is a success because the relationship developed transcends the technology deployed.

> The relationship developed transcends the technology deployed.

There are many areas in which the use of technology to speed processing has helped my life and yours. When I'm renting from Hertz, I find its Hertz Gold service to be terrific. The bus drops you off, and you find your name in lights over your assigned car. Quickly, you get in and drive away. It's speedy, it's efficient, and it is a differentiating factor.

Are you starting to get used to the self-service kiosks at airports? I am—albeit somewhat reluctantly. Yet, the kiosk is certainly an advantage when you're running late and need to get to your flight. And, given the quality of the conversation with the ticket agent mentioned previously, the kiosk is certainly as user-friendly.

It really doesn't seem all that long ago you would apply for a loan, and then nervously wait for several days to discover whether or not you had been approved. Processing loans has certainly changed, thanks to technology.

Household, a Fortune 200 company with a 120-year history, lends money for auto purchases through its Household Finance Corporation division. The speed with which a dealer can respond regarding financing can be the difference between gaining or losing the sale—and Household wanted to be responsive to the five thousand–plus auto dealers with whom it has relationships. But it also needed to integrate any new technology with the data it had developed as far back as the 1980s. As IBM documents on one of its Web sites, its E-bridge solution provided Household with the ability to grow loan volume—without proportionally increasing staff and administrative costs—and "move the loan application review process from days to minutes."[2]

It's important to note, however, that Household also suggests the main reason this is so important is that the technology gave the company the opportunity to "grow relationships."

Note a similarity here?

Speed in processing is of value to the organization *only* when the customer *doesn't* feel *processed*!

Processing Strategies. How do you process customers without them *feeling* processed? There are really some simple steps that cost any business practically *zero* dollars, and will help you provide what customers REALLY want.

Here are just four ideas to make processing more palatable for your customers:

1. *Use the customer's name as often as possible.* If you have the client's name in front of you—or if you can easily ask it—why not use it? It costs you nothing and makes the transaction processing infinitely more personal.

2. *Don't focus on the speed of the transaction so much that it becomes dehumanizing.* Remember in the movie *Top Gun* when Maverick and Goose say in unison their famous line, "I feel the need—the need for speed!"? Good advice for fighter pilots; bad strategy for building customer relationships.

   Don't get me wrong—no one wants to wait one second longer than necessary! However, no customer wants to feel as if he's been given the "bum's rush," either. Yet, because speed of transaction is easier to measure than friendliness of transaction or thoroughness of transaction (more on this later), we focus on making things move quicker for our customers. Some organizations do this to the point that the customer feels like a number—and when the customer feels processed in that way, he or she will not reward you with unwavering loyalty.

3. *Use humor when appropriate.* Perhaps this could be better expressed, "Use *appropriate* humor when appropriate." In other words, spicing up the interaction with a bit of fun helps build customer relationships. The most overused example of this is Southwest Airlines and the humor its flight attendants use before, during, and after departure.

(I was on a Southwest flight a while back that had an extraordinarily rough landing—in fact, it was bone jarring! The flight attendant came on the intercom and calmly said, "And now, while our pilot taxis *what is left* of our aircraft to the gate . . . we'd like to thank you for flying Southwest!")

Just a little bit of fun goes a long way in creating a feeling that your employees are not just processing your customers and prospects by rote. However, don't forget that in today's "politically correct" and hypersensitive times, all humor must be appropriate to the situation.

4. *Make the wait part of the experience.* No one likes standing in line to check in to a hotel—yet at the Mirage in Las Vegas, the amazing aquarium behind the front desk is hypnotic and makes your wait an enjoyable part of the experience. At Mandalay Bay, beautifully costumed women walk up to you in line and show you the incredibly colorful parrots they carry.

How can you make the line—the wait—customers may have to endure a positive part of the total process of doing business with you?

In the June 9, 2003, *Forbes* magazine, the story "Funny Business" by Monte Burke outlined how Bank of America—the nation's largest consumer bank—executes all of these strategies. On "Hawaiian Fridays," employees don grass skirts, communicate personally, and—believe it or not—form conga lines with the customers waiting for a teller. As the article says, "At Bank of America these antics are the result of mandatory 'spirit training.'" According to the article, Bank of America insists customer satisfaction is soaring. I would suggest a significant reason for this is that when they process customers, the customers do not *feel* processed.

How do *your* customers feel?

Level Two: Customer Service

"Thank you for calling the XYZ Company. We appreciate your call. We are committed to the highest standards of customer service. Our customer service representatives are busy caring for other customers right now. You will be connected with the next available customer service representative."

Does this sound familiar to you?

Boring background music plays for about ten seconds; then you hear, "We are receiving a higher-than-expected number of calls. Please be advised that your wait for a customer service representative will exceed twenty minutes."

What!? Are you kidding me? What a bunch of liars these XYZ guys are, right? (And I do not use the word *liar* here without some forethought!) If they were really and truly "committed to the highest standards of customer service," they wouldn't make you wait twenty minutes to talk to someone!

One cellular telephone company I deal with has had a recording on their customer service line for *two years* saying that they are receiving a "higher-than-expected call volume." Shouldn't someone—anyone—reexamine the *expected* call volume?

We've reached Level Two: customer service. What exactly *is* customer service, anyway?

I searched for definitions of "customer service" on Google, and here are some that I found, with my comments to follow in parentheses:

- "Activities and programs provided by the seller to make the relationship a satisfying one for the customer." (Basic, but not bad, huh? But remember what we said about the true value of "satisfaction" . . .)—from the Web site of the Northern Colleges Network in the United Kingdom

- "The activities that support orders, including application, advice, configuration, order processing, handling, post-sale communication and special services. The primary objective of customer service is to increase customer satisfaction, operational efficiency and customer loyalty." (Does this one sound to you like a committee wrote it?)—from the consulting company FiveTwelve Group's Web site

- "The degree of assistance and courtesy granted those who patronize the organization." (Usually when dealing with customer service issues, expect the "degree of assistance" to be the third degree.)—from the National Business Research Institute Web site

- "The area of the company that provides product information, help and/or technical support to new customers and sells them the products or services they need or want." (This one made my blood boil!) —from the "Business Trouble Shooter" Web site of Halverson-Quigley Management Systems

All you have to do is read these definitions to begin to understand the basic problem with the level and quality of customer service that is driving your clients nuts! Every statement I've listed—and the ones I haven't—talks about "activities" and "programs" and "degree(s) of assistance." *None* talked about the *values* or *commitment* or *mission* of a business to its customers.

One of the definitions cited here even restricts customer service to "the *area* of the company"—as if *only* that individual division or area was responsible for—and responsive to—the needs of customers!

By the way, certainly I'm in a minority for thinking this, but I absolutely hate that line about "exceeding customer expectations." Most customers have been so used and abused that their expectations are minimal. So, you're going to "exceed customer expectations"? Not placing the bar too high for yourself, are you?

Let's face it: "exceeding customer expectations" is a meaningless cliché. Have you really, truly evaluated the expectations of your customers? What is their range of expectations? How have you measured whether the fulfillment of their most demanding expectations makes financial sense for your organization? To what degree are you going to "exceed expectations"? One percent? How will you know when you've been successful and—more important—when you haven't?

Customers—no matter what your business produces—are your very reason for existence! In the May 27, 2003, *Fortune* magazine article by Adam Lashinsky on new therapies being developed for cancer, one medical entrepreneur commented that his company existed to receive FDA approval for its unique approach to chemotherapy. I understand what he's saying—and why he's saying it. And I realize you can't get to customers in that business without FDA approval. Yet it seems to me that all the FDA's approval does is allow the company to proceed and attempt to become a force in the marketplace by helping patients (read "customers") defeat their cancer and prolong their lives. FDA approval without customers means bankrupt business. In other words, this company should be existing to save the lives of their customers, not to receive government certification.

To return to the earlier point, the aforementioned definitions of customer service are so illustrative of the problems, because they lack the gut-level commitment that any organization must have to its customers to truly serve them at the level they desire.

Here is one of the primary reasons: measurement.

I'm serious. *Measurement* is preventing organizations from making significant progression in enhancing levels of customer service.

Remember the old saw "If all you have is a hammer, every problem appears to be a nail"? It's the same principle here. We say, "We can't manage what we can't measure." So, guess what organizations do? Instead of basing their definitions of service around what customers REALLY want, they base them around the improvement of only *those activities that are measurable.*

It's tough to measure the friendliness of the drive-thru employee, so service is determined to be the speed at which the customer is served. That's easily timed and, therefore, easily measured. But think about it: Would you drive through a fast-food restaurant that had a sign that said, "Surly service—but we're quick!"?

Airlines cannot measure compassion to passengers, but they can measure if the plane left the gate on time. Therefore, you find yourself sprinting through Atlanta. The airline knows your connecting flight was late and that you are hustling your way to their gate—yet they close the door and pull the Jetway back so they can keep what is being measured (on-time departure) on track . . . even at the risk of alienating a customer.

The Customer Satisfaction Measurement Association lists as one of their objectives "To support the use of benchmarking to facilitate process improvement and the achievement of superior customer satisfaction." Now, *please* don't misunderstand the point here: I'm not suggesting for a moment that benchmarking and measurement aren't necessary—even vital. However, shouldn't we at least ask if our measurements have caused us to make our definition—and, therefore, our execution—of customer service strategies prejudiced toward those activities that lend themselves to being measured?

Let's take the furniture industry as an example of the problems with measurement. America's Research Group—a well-respected research organization founded by its visionary CEO, Britt Beemer—surveyed approximately five thousand shoppers nationwide regarding their furniture shopping plans for the coming year. In the study, 84 percent of American consumers responded that they can't measure quality in upholstery. Two-thirds said that they can't measure quality in case goods. Since most of the "guts" of the furniture product are hidden from view, customers stated that they can't see inside to assess the true quality of the product.

So, how do customers determine value? By how they *feel* about the furniture. How do you measure "customer service" to those customers when they are evaluating *you* by their feelings?

In *Competitive Intelligence and Measurement in Organizational Research,* a research paper published online by the University of Pittsburgh School of Business, Dr. Yogesh Malhotra writes, "Measurement may be defined as the process of determining the value or level, either qualitative or quantitative, of a particular attribute for a particular unit of analysis. In organizational research, the unit of analysis may be the individual, the group, or the organization itself." Got it?

Now, I am certain that Dr. Malhotra is exactly right about measurement from a clinical, intellectual point of view. And there's no doubt that is vital to the success of any business. However, I would suggest that the best step you can take is to change your *thinking*. If your measurement focuses on Level One activities, then you are *not* measuring "customer service"! You are measuring your success at customer *processing*.

In his book, *Avoiding the Customer Service Rut*, Fredrik Dahlsten—a researcher at MIT/Chalmers University of Technology in Sweden and market intelligence manager at Volvo—clearly demonstrates how customer satisfaction can become distorted by selecting the wrong variables to measure—and then using that "wrong" information in reactive ways.

Through his study and practical experience, Dahlsten concludes that companies and managers should measure quality—but *focus* on creating positive, emotional customer *experiences*.

You need to realize that customers want—and expect—your organization to provide them Level One in a timely, efficient, and consistent manner. They want the processing that exists in just about any business situation—from paying at the checkout counter to receiving a monthly statement—to be accurate and well organized. As customers, we understand that there is always going to be the element of processing. We just don't want it to be the sum of our relationship.

Customers want you to get it right, not make it right!

It's important to note that you cannot build loyalty and significant relationships with customers if you cannot perform at Level One. If I have to stand in line for an hour, or my bill is incorrect, or you constantly put the wrong sandwich in my bag, or telephone calls aren't returned promptly, why should I even give you a chance to gain additional business?

We're all human—there's no doubt that occasionally mistakes will be made. Yet many companies focus on the "making it right to the customer" aspect to the point that it excuses and enables sloppy behavior in dealing with customers. If your focus is on *making* it right," why would an employee make a valiant effort to *get* it right?

Make that an organizational mantra: *Customers want you to* get *it right, not* make *it right!* (Making it right is preferred to nothing at all—yet you're only going to get so many chances.)

Relationship Means "Reciprocal." In your personal life, here's something you certainly realize: a relationship is valid only when more than one party is involved. If you love someone who won't have anything to do with you . . . well, that's not a "relationship." (Sometimes it's called "stalking.")

The same is true in business—you have a relationship with a customer only when both you *and* your customer are involved.

This simple fact should cause us to consider all the billions of dollars spent on customer relationship management (CRM)—and ask if it is getting a reasonable return on this massive investment.

A BearingPoint study on customers in financial services found that despite the CRM efforts, "only 22 percent of financial service executives believe their customers would actively promote their services to their family and friends."[3] If, after all this time and money and effort, you can only get a referral rate of less than one-fourth, you have to question whether or not we really understand what "relationship management" means.

That moves us to Level Two—after you've processed the customer correctly, he asks, "Now what?" In other words, how will you prove by your actions that service to your customers is part of the very fabric of your organization?

If I'm shuttled off to the "area of the company that provides product information, help and/or technical support to new customers and sells them the products or services they need or want"—well, does that sound like a commitment to a true relationship? "Our area provides help and support for our products—and then sells the poor suckers something else." Hardly the stuff of which loyal, committed customers are made.

Customers want to know that you are so committed to them, you will provide service above and beyond mere processing. Yet, if you're measuring the wrong thing, you will obviously obtain the wrong answer.

A CEO friend of mine and I were discussing this concept in a recent telephone conversation in which he experienced something I call the "blinding flash of the obvious." He told me he could recount scores of meetings where research was presented regarding studies that evaluated various aspects of his company's efforts in customer service. He said, "You know, I don't think anyone at any point in any meeting ever stopped the discussion and asked, 'Are we *sure* that this is what our clients REALLY want from us?' And," he continued, "I find that terrifying." The important question is, are you terrified enough to ask that question in a meeting at *your* organization?

Level Two—customer service—should mean that your organization has a commitment to taking the way you treat your clients a level above mere processing. It means you've pledged as a department, company, or business that you'll meet a higher standard . . . and understand it is a standard that the customer, not you, will determine.

Yet this standard—as defined by the customer—is constantly changing . . . and getting tougher.

In *Nation's Restaurant News*, Nick Garvey, vice president of training for the Dallas, Texas, company named Consolidated Restaurant Companies—whose concepts include Spaghetti Warehouse and El Chico—says, "The bar has been raised. The ability to deliver a $50-per-person experience at a $15-per-person average will allow us to propel ourselves in growth. I think Houston's (restaurants) figured that out years ago." That's why Garvey's company began implementing the service procedures found in its three fine-dining restaurants into its casual-concept restaurants—the thirty-unit Spaghetti Warehouse and sixty-three-unit El Chico.

But there's the problem: How do you deliver $50 service to a $15 customer?

Answer? You don't. You have to move from Level Two—customer *service*—to Level Three—what customers REALLY want—a customer *experience*.

Level Three: Customer Experience

Did you notice in the previous quote that the restaurant training executive did *not* use the word *service?* He chose the term *experience*—and with good reason.

The customer experience is that powerful feeling generated when the processing goes right, the service is impeccable—*and* there is a compelling emotional element that engages the customer. It means you've knocked it out of the park in both Level One and Level Two, but you've done more than handle and assist—you've *moved* the customer.

The airline company jetBlue is a great example of a business that moves its customers (pardon the pun). Not just from one airport to another, but in the manner in which it creates a customer experience. So much so, in fact, that customers practically wax poetic about them. Consider this example from "The Motley Fool," where columnist Whitney Tilson writes regarding the airline:

> Consistently delivering an exceptionally positive customer experience is the key to long-term business success in *any* industry. Doing so, however, is extremely complex and difficult. Yet once achieved, it can feed on itself, creating a virtuous cycle and becoming a powerful competitive advantage—one that can be very difficult for competitors to match. JetBlue clearly understands this and the results show.

He continues, "I'm convinced that it is not only the greatest airline I've ever encountered, but one of the finest businesses in the world. Seriously."[4]

Several reports about jetBlue quote CEO David Neeleman and what he describes as his mission: "The very simple goal of bringing humanity back to air travel." As one of Tilson's columns notes, "Humanity. Notice Neeleman didn't say, 'Bringing low fares and good service back to air travel.' He said, in effect, that most airlines treat their customers in an inhumane fashion and that he was determined that jetBlue would be 'a different kind of airline.'"

In other words, jetBlue recognizes that—to paraphrase an earlier example—it's not about the plane. It's about the people—employees and customers—inside it. This understanding, and the execution of strategies like DirecTV at every seat, proves they "get it." They engage customers and create a passenger experience that resonates far more than mere service.

This is clearly a powerful strategy—jetBlue's results show it has a healthy balance sheet (especially for the airline industry) and is generating profit, positive cash flow, *and* a lower ticket price and higher revenue per flight than even Southwest. Some aviation experts suggest that jetBlue may someday become the dominant airline in the country.

The customer experience created by Southwest Airlines has been well documented and perhaps overly discussed. We should note, however, that Southwest differentiated itself from other airlines through the unique experience it created for its customers. Flight attendants entertaining passengers with jokes about air travel, peanuts as the sole food on every flight for many years, no assigned seats—these were all distinctive when introduced by Southwest; jetBlue understood that it could not simply repeat what Southwest was doing—it had to find a way to differentiate. If you've flown jetBlue, you know that it *is* a different experience from flying Southwest.

In each case the plane still takes you from Florida to New York. You still get processed and you still get served, no matter which airline you fly. Yet these two highly successful companies in the same industry can differentiate themselves from each other (and the rest of the pack) by the individual experience each respectively provides.

As you seek to move to Level Three, your biggest challenge may come from within your organization—not from the customers you seek to engage.

In a 2003 study conducted on customer-driven business performance by the American Management Association, Braun Consulting and Deep Customer Connections, announced results that indicated "that the most formidable challenges for marketers actually lie within their own organizations: developing inter-unit cooperation, effecting change, and leading integrated corporate-wide initiatives. However, marketers indicated that they realize one of their most important roles is to provide the leadership to foster the organizational alignment that is required for implementing customer-centric strategies across the enterprise."[5]

Of course, that shouldn't come as a surprise when there is—at least in some organizations, as evidenced by the previously cited definitions—a perception that customers are the responsibility of particular "areas" or departments of the company. If only certain segments of the company are customer focused, how does that business develop interdepartmental cooperation, make change really happen, and integrate initiatives? Answer: it can't. Well . . . let me place a condition on that— it *could*, if that business had the kind of leadership within the organization that would make it possible. Yet, if the business still considers customer processing, service, and experience to be compartmentalized, let's face it—the leadership is probably out to lunch anyway.

Tim Sanders, Leadership Coach of Yahoo, describes it very well: "Organizations need to deliver not only high-quality products and services, but also staged experiences that are dramatic and engaging. It's no longer about highlighting benefits—it's about creating sensations."[6]

But for most managers, there's the rub. How much of your training and experience in business has been geared toward the creation of sensations? (A CFO friend of mine told me the only sensations he had been trained to create were fear and loathing!)

We have now reached a fundamental disconnect:

- What business describes as *service* (Level Two), most customers feel is *processing* (Level One).

- What business describes as an *experience* (Level Three), most customers feel is *service* (Level Two).

- What customers REALLY want is *experience* (Level Three), and most businesses and their managers don't have a clue how to create it, because it is totally outside the framework of the organization and the skill set of the professional.

What Are the Elements of a Customer Experience? First, you execute at Level One and Level Two in an exemplary manner. If you aren't getting

mere processing and service right, your efforts at Level Three are falling on deaf ears.

Obviously, that's not as easy as it sounds. Many organizations are still hung up at this point—making the move to Level Three irrelevant until they get their acts together. If the line is unbearably long and the wrong food is placed in my bag, it really doesn't matter what "sensations" (to use Tim Sanders's phrase) you create. You've lost me.

If you have to fix Levels One and Two, then do it—and do it now! You cannot create the differentiating experiences that customers really want until you do.

So what separates Level Three from the other two?

There are many variables and many philosophies; however, I would suggest it comes down to this: The organization that creates Level Three is the one that combines this trio of elements:

1. Superior information

2. Systematic empathy

3. An obsession for sensation

Superior Information

The Level Three organization just flat-out knows more about its customers than those dwelling in Level Two. It makes amazing efforts to know its customer's wants and needs. Yet this organization also goes the next step and seeks to discover more about the customer than is necessary to make a mere sale.

Superior information does not mean you know that a certain percentage of your customers prefer, for example, investments with a moderate risk as opposed to high risk. Superior information means you know specifically *which* clients have that preference. You know their names—and you know *why* they feel the way they do.

At a Merrill Lynch conference I was addressing in Florida, I entered the meeting room as a presenter from Accenture Consulting was finishing his talk. I don't remember his name, but I will never forget what he said. In a study on UBS—a competitor to Merrill that has a dominant share of Europe's "ultra"-high net worth clients—he said that Accenture discovered some pretty remarkable steps that UBS had taken with its European clients.

UBS certainly wanted to know everything it could discover about its clients' financial situations. However, it discovered that what it had learned above and beyond the monetary that created the experiences that engendered loyalty. As an example, the company wanted to know what its top clients' favorite artists were. Why? So when that very wealthy individual came to an appointment with his UBS financial adviser, replicas of his or her favorite artist's paintings were hanging in the conference room.

Advisers also wanted to know what sports the children of their clients were playing. Why? So the financial adviser could purchase a subscription to a magazine about that particular sport, and have it sent directly to the child.

The point of all this, according to the consultant, was that UBS wanted its clients to know it cared more about them than their money. "And," he continued, "you cannot do that unless you have superior information. Information about the things that most professionals would not think matters."

Does your organization really know more about your customers than your competition does?

I know my best client's favorite wine is Duckhorn. He is a true wine connoisseur, and no doubt is enamored with other, rarer vintages, but if he had to pick a preferred brand to consume regularly, it would be Duckhorn.

The important point is, I don't know that *because* he's my best client. It is because I know this (and a whole lot more) that he and his organization *became* my best client.

Benjamin Franklin once said, "The sweetest sound in any language is a man's own name." I believe in today's business world, the sweetest sound—and a true force in the creation of Level Three—is the sentence or two when someone expresses that they care enough to know what really matters to you.

But one caveat: use your knowledge with subtlety and restraint. The best way to let your clients and prospects know that you have superior information is to show them—not tell them. A bottle of Duckhorn as a gift says the right things. To tell the client, "I know your children's names, your favorite artist, preferred wine, and more" says all the wrong things. I'm certain that UBS advisers do not grandly point to the frames on the wall and say, "LOOK! Your favorite artist!" They don't have to; the fact that they are hanging there says it all.

Systematic Empathy

Sounds like an oxymoron, doesn't it? When you make empathy a part of the system, isn't there the risk of robbing it of its impact?

Of course.

What I am suggesting here is to make it a part of the "corporate DNA" that your policy is one of empathy toward the customer before loyalty to internal policy and procedure.

Encarta World English Dictionary defines *empathy* as "The ability to identify with and understand another person's feelings or difficulties." What customer wouldn't want that from the place where she does business?

My buddy Larry Winget—one of the nation's finest professional speakers—recounts to his audiences a bad customer experience he suffered while shopping at a national retail chain. Invariably, when he relates in his story that he was told by a clerk that something couldn't be done for him because "it wasn't company . . ."—without fail, the entire audience responds with the word *"policy"*!

We've all heard it! "It's not our policy to do that." "No, we do not allow substitutions to the menu." "Sorry, we just don't do it that way." (Larry's retort to that is to respond, "Congratulations. Now you're going to get the chance!")

The examples of the wonderful execution of this principle of systematic empathy at Ritz-Carlton hotels are numerous. One of the points I've noticed is that their staff will almost always respond to a request with these two words: "No problem!" Please note—this isn't just a "nice" phrase to train your employees to say. They have to execute this as a principle of the organization. "No problem" means we empathize that your request has value. "No problem" means we put the person before policy.

However, here's the important point: "No problem" *is* the policy! It makes empathy systematic and systemic in the culture!

Obviously, situations must be handled in a manner that is legal, ethical, and responsible. Perhaps the best test is this one: Given that aforementioned parameter, if an employee varied from your organization's official policy to amaze and delight a customer, would she be praised or punished?

Here's the second-best test: If the policy was violated, would you first be concerned with the customer—or the violation? Would you even ask the customer if this action by your employee had a positive impact—or would you merely be concerned as a manager that someone stepped "outside the box"?

When you create a customer experience—and move your interactions to Level Three—you create the ultimate competitive advantage.

I recently spoke to the W. W. Williams Company at a meeting in Cleveland. (By the way, to create an enjoyable aspect for their meeting, part of it was held at the Rock and Roll Hall of Fame!) As their Web site (www.wwwilliams.com) states, "Founded in Columbus, Ohio, in 1912, W. W. Williams has become one of the nation's oldest and largest industrial distribution firms, continually growing across the country incorporating new facilities, new ideas, and new expertise. We represent and service some of the most advanced and innovative diesel engine, automatic transmission, power generation and transport refrigeration technologies currently on the market."

Notice the early part of that statement talks about "industrial distribution," while the latter segment states their work in "service." Because of strategic changes by Daimler Chrysler in its method of distribution, a significant portion of the revenue of this particular division of the company was being severely impacted. In a discussion during the meeting, where managers were voicing their difficulties in dealing with this problem, one manager—who ran one of Williams's combination distribution units and repair centers for diesel engines—spoke up and announced that his business was up by a significant percentage!

The reason? He stated that he realized his customers' trucks weren't breaking down in his shop—they were breaking down at his customers' points of business. So he called his customers and asked if he could place his mechanics in *their* locations so they wouldn't have to worry about bringing the trucks into the Williams location for repairs. The result was reduced downtime for his customers—and amazing returns for Williams.

That's not just mere "service"—it is the display of empathy for the customer, which creates a compelling experience that develops amazing client loyalty.

As mentioned earlier, regardless of your personal political persuasion, when Bill Clinton said that he "felt the pain" of the American people, he did something most politicians are not able to do: He displayed empathy in a manner that resonated with his "customers." How are you putting that principle into action at your organization? I would argue that empathy involves the display of your legitimate concern for others through the action you take to ensure that they benefit from a relationship with you. In other words, empathy is more than just talk. It is the meaningful display to your customers that you "feel their pain"—and will take the steps to assist them in its resolution. When your employees do this based on their individual personalities and commitment, it is just "empathy." When the organization not only condones it but also makes it a matter of high priority, then it is "systematic empathy."

An Obsession for Sensation

As I write this, I have a friend in a hospital in Louisville. Cardiac surgeons have just transplanted an artificial heart into his chest cavity.

To say that I am stunned by this development is a gross understatement. Here is a guy who had Easter lunch with his wife in my home in Las Vegas a mere two weeks ago. Now an artificial pump is keeping him alive—and, at this point, he's responding amazingly well.

When my wife talked with his, she asked the obvious question: "Why was Don willing to do this?" The answer was profound. His wife simply said, "He felt the doctors really cared about him."

Don's willingness to go through the procedure—with all of its obvious risks, pain, and challenge—wasn't based on his commitment to the advancement of the treatment of heart disease. (Although, knowing him as I do, I don't doubt this factor also played an important role.) It was because of his feeling that the doctors cared about him—and that they viewed him as more than a science project. They wanted him to *live*—not just to experiment on a human being with an amazing piece of technology.

Dr. Bill Beeson—one of the nation's premier cosmetic surgeons and a close personal friend—recently told me about a conference on malpractice insurance, a subject that is obviously a major concern in the health-care industry. According to Dr. Beeson, a senior officer in an insurance company asked the doctors, "You know why you're getting sued? Because your patients don't like you." In other words, doctors being sued are often the ones who have an obsession with medicine—but *not* with the sensations he or she creates for the patient and his or her recovery.

Dr. Elliott B. Jaffa teaches a course on several "distance learning" programs—including the Internet-based African Virtual University, an intergovernmental organization based in Nairobi, Kenya, with more than thirty-four learning centers in seventeen African countries—entitled "Customer Obsession." Dr. Jaffa states in his course description something we've already discussed—that customer obsession is not the same as customer service. He then asks students to take a "Customer Obsession Test" back to their organizations. To paraphrase Dr. Jaffa, students should ask the following questions about their businesses:

- Does your organization think "customer" whenever you make a decision or establish a policy?

- Does the customer feel better served than he/she expected?

- Does your organization create a perception of value received—making the customer feel good about doing business with you?

- Have you made your business one big customer experience department that expands your business, cross-sells, and secures new business?

- Do you treat your customers as if you were going to see them every working day for the rest of your life? And . . . that at the end of *each* visit the customer would then decide to buy something from either you or one of your competitors?

Lucent Technologies understands that an obsession for customers creates an important link—and the sensations that create a customer experience are usually established through the *people* on the front lines of your organization. That's why they cosponsor a distance learning initiative called the Alliance Program. Lucent installers and other occupational employees in their installation area are provided with an opportune way to earn an associate, bachelor's, or master's degree in a variety of disciplines, including telecommunications, mathematics, business, and psychology, through this program.[7]

"For many of our customers, installers are the only physical contact they have with Lucent," said Ed Janas, Customer Service Vice President—Installation West. "By providing those installers with additional education and skills in their field, installers are better able to serve customers. This leaves the customers with a positive impression of Lucent, which could lead to future business opportunities with that customer and others. That's what Lucent is all about—increasing our growth *through our obsession with customers.*"

Notice how these two tie together? When you start asking the questions suggested by Dr. Jaffa, you realize that your organization has to develop the obsession for creating sensations with your customers through the frontline, grassroots employees of your business. If you're a bank, that means the teller—not just the branch manager. If you're Lucent, it means the installer—not just the sales professional. If you're an entrepreneur, it means YOU—it is not enough to merely have a personal obsession for your product.

Starbucks is obsessed with the sensations its customers receive when they walk in the door. Disney is obsessed with the sensations its visitors experience when they enter the theme park. Harrah's is obsessed with the sensations of its guests when they arrive at the casino. And Pyramid

Coach is obsessed with the sensations our artists receive when they board the bus.

As my good friend Tim Wilmott, chief operating officer of Harrah's, told me, "We have to be obsessed with customers. Think about it: most of the people who do business with us have the expectation that they may *lose money* being our customer! We have to make them feel good about it!" Don't get Tim Wilmott wrong—what he means here is that although you may lose a few bucks (or more) gambling at one of the many Harrah's casinos, the sensations that its wonderfully obsessed team has worked to create for you will make you want to return. My point is that if a company like Harrah's can do this when many of its customers lose money by doing business there, how can any of us demand less of our organizations?

How obsessed are you—and your business—about the sensations *your* customers receive?

Executive Summary

The First Disconnection is that customers REALLY want a "compelling experience"—yet most organizations provide them with "customer service."

- The main reason for this disconnection is that organizations often do not consider that there are three levels of customer interaction:
  - Level One: *Customer Processing*

    Processing is the most basic stage of customer interaction. It is the simple "blocking and tackling" that gets the customer through the process of transaction with your organization. It can most often be precisely measured by the speed and/or accuracy of the transaction.
  - Level Two: *Customer Service*

    Customer service is most often thought of as the effort by your organization to provide support to your clients, as well as make the transaction go more smoothly. Many organizations mistakenly believe that customer service can be delegated to distinct areas of the company, rather than become a pervasive part of the mission and culture of the business.

○ Level Three: *Customer Experience*

Customer experience is the creation of emotional connections and sensations with customers and prospects through the use of superior information and systematic empathy within the organization to create encounters that will engender loyalty from the customer.

- The single most significant problem is that organizations and customers are defining their interactions differently.

  ○ What many organizations are terming as "customer service" is, in fact, "customer processing."

  ○ What many organizations are terming as "customer experience" is, instead, merely "customer service."

  ○ What customers are seeking—the "customer experience"—is outside of the training, skill set, and ability of many professionals because of their training, background, and approach to business relationships.

- There are three major aspects to creating a compelling customer experience:

  ○ *Superior information*

    - It is not just knowing more about your customer base in general: superior information means you know which specific customers have what individual preferences.

29

- This means you not only know their product and / or service desires and needs, you know their individual preferences, as well.

○ *Systematic empathy*

- Is responding to the needs of customers systemic in your organization? For companies that can answer this question in the affirmative, their employees know that they can take the steps necessary to create a compelling experience for customers on the spot.

- These organizations constantly respond not merely to "exceed customer expectations" but instead to develop a compelling partnership with the customer for mutual benefit and to enhance a long-term reciprocal relationship.

○ *An obsession for sensation*

- Organizations with an obsession for sensation are constantly proving to their customers that they care more for them than their money. By doing so, they create long-term relationships that are more financially beneficial than a mere succession of transactions.

- These wonderfully obsessed organizations make their business into one big "customer experience department" that expands business, cross-sells, and secures new customers.

- Visionary businesses—such as Harrah's, Starbucks, and (on a much smaller scale) local physicians and small-town grocery stores as cited in this chapter—create a feeling of passion and excitement from their customers . . . who reward those organizations with loyalty and referrals. They treat their customers as if they were going to see them every working day for the rest of their lives.

Bridge Building
Moving from Customer Service to Compelling Experience

- Who in your organization would handle a customer's problem the way that Hertz handled mine? How can you make that kind of behavior a part of your system of customer interaction?

- We've learned that perhaps the worst response we can get from customers is indifference. What are you doing to prevent customer apathy?

- Outline your organization's performance in the Three Stages of Customer Interaction:
  - *Processing*
  - *Service*
  - *Experience*

- What steps can you take to enhance the efficiency of processing—while at the same time ensuring it does not detract from the experience?

- What do you think the difference is between "service" and "experience" at your organization? Remember that emotion plays a critical role . . . so how are you bringing emotion into the relationships you have with customers?

- In this chapter you read several definitions of customer service—what's *yours*?

- Is customer interaction considered the role of a specific department in your organization? Does *everyone* realize the importance of customers?

- Are you measuring what is important in building customer experiences—or are you measuring what is easier to measure?
  - Are you discussing the aspects of customer interaction that are vital but cannot be instantaneously measured? (Note: This is where the measurement of customer loyalty comes in to play.)

- Do you find yourself spending more time getting it right or making it right for customers?
- Specifically describe where you have superior information about your customers compared to your competition.
- How is empathy a part of the natural manner in which you interface with customers?
- Outline how your organization is obsessed with creating compelling sensations for customers.

2

THE SECOND DISCONNECTION

What Customers REALLY Want: *Personal Focus*
What Business Supplies: *Product Focus*

In the Salesman's Office

As I sat in the car salesman's office, the thought suddenly struck me that I had now learned more about the new BMW Z4 than I ever really wanted to know.

I'm sorry, but I really don't care about the 98.2-inch wheelbase and that it tracks at 58 inches in the front and 60 in the rear. I'm not sure I really know what the term *tracks* means. I guess the 14.5-gallon fuel tank combined with the gas mileage of 21 in the city and 28 on the highway is good. But it really wasn't important to me.

Did I mention the car weighs 2,998 pounds? The salesman certainly did. Sure, he could've rounded it to an even 3,000, but he was trying to make an impact.

If he was trying to impress me with his product knowledge, he succeeded.

If he was trying to impress me with his focus on the customer, he was a miserable failure.

In my first book, I wrote about the wonderful, amazing experience I had buying a BMW from Carl Nielsen at Dryer & Reinbold BMW in Indianapolis. Perhaps my expectations were too high when I visited a

BMW dealership in a city in the west where I had relocated. However, I believe what really happened is that Carl provides what his customers REALLY want—and the guy in the other dealership didn't have a clue.

Philippe Suchet, CEO of consulting firm Kefta, Inc., wrote "As a marketer or product manager, your goal is to sell your company's product or service. Most approach this task by making their product visible to the largest number of people possible. This is often a flawed approach."[1] As my experience at the BMW dealership proved to me, Suchet is exactly right.

In the Words of Alec Baldwin

One of my favorite movies is the film adaptation of David Mamet's Pulitzer Prize–winning play, *Glengarry Glen Ross*. In this 1992 production, a group of real estate salesmen struggle with a significant downturn in the market—and the pressures of sales. The salesmen in the film are made up of one of the most superb casts ever assembled, including Al Pacino, Kevin Spacey, Ed Harris, Alan Arkin, and the great Jack Lemmon, in one of his finest performances. Yet even with this incredible group of actors, the film really becomes electric upon the arrival of Alec Baldwin.

Baldwin plays a character named Blake, the corporate "motivator." As such, he gives a presentation that is one of the great moments in film. While his speech—and the entire movie—seems to be attempting to make profanity an art form, he nonetheless is terrifying as he informs the salesmen of a new contest he is instituting. The contest is that any salesman who doesn't obtain his quota of leads is fired. (How's *that* for motivation?)

In his memorable talk, Blake cites the acronym "ABC." As he intensely projects his point, Blake/Baldwin repeats, "ABC. *Always Be Closing.*"

Part of this production's power is that we feel such compassion for these men trapped in such a horrible situation. Yet, at the same time, we're repulsed by the tricks and tactics they use to sell their product to unsuspecting and somewhat defenseless customers.

I was thinking about this film as I contemplated the disconnection that customers have with many organizations. I wonder if the BMW salesman in the western dealership I visited had been told to "always be closing." I wonder if he ever considered the concept that maybe the focus *shouldn't* be on the car. Maybe he should have thought—or some sales manager should have taught him—that ancient line from sales training: "Customers do not buy your product; they buy what your product will do for them."

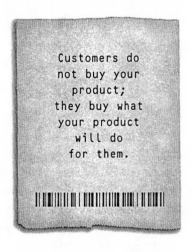

Customers do not buy your product; they buy what your product will do for them.

Was I really buying a BMW Z4? Not really. I was seeking a convertible that I could enjoy year-round now that I was living in the West, rather than in Indiana. BMW Financing had created a terrific experience for me, so I wanted to work with them again. And I thought the design of the new Z4 was very sharp. So, as much as I hate to admit it, I wanted—here in my midlife crisis—to look "cool."

Maybe my salesman at BMW could've found that out if he had focused on his customer rather than his product.

Organizations today are collectively spending billions of dollars to build their brands—yet what we really want is a personal focus on our needs as the customer, not a product focus on a brand. As Regis McKenna, the renowned marketing sage, says, "Choice has become a higher value than brand in America."

My guess is that my ineffective BMW salesman was butting up against the two main reasons that many salespeople focus on their products and services rather than on those who consume them. These two rationales I will suggest undoubtedly sound simplistic, but when you examine the reality of the manner in which most organizations communicate with their customers, there is no denying that they play a powerful role. And, it is important to note, this is not just about how professionals sell your products and services—it is about the philosophy, the culture, of your organization. Consider these two factors that contribute to a product-centered focus:

1. It's easier.
2. We're desperate.

It's Easier

It is! It is easier to focus on the product rather than the customer—and a huge percentage of human beings (maybe 100 percent!) will attempt to take the path of least resistance.

Let's take our cargo trailers business at Obsidian Enterprises as an example. At United Trailer—and our recently acquired Classic Trailer—we build pretty basic cargo trailers as a part of our product line. These are the trailers you would haul your "stuff" in, that a landscaping company might use to carry mowers and other equipment, or that a motorcyclist might use to transport his bike somewhere.

Our engineers work to make these trailers easy for our customers to use—and reliable, as well. Employees of United and Classic have many decades of experience in designing, manufacturing, and marketing these trailers—and have done so with a great deal of success.

So . . . what's the problem?

The problem is that when a customer wants a trailer, it is infinitely easier for us to talk about our trailer than listen to the customer! It seems so much more efficient to explain our features and benefits than to examine her specific situation. It goes so far in some companies (hopefully none of ours!) that it appears they are saying, "If you don't understand how our superior product works, then you don't deserve to own one!"

If you communicate with your customers in this manner, then it's easy—you have only one story to learn! It's the story of your product.

My friend Ron Karr of Karr Associates tells of his initial selling experiences: "From my early days selling copiers, I can remember having to memorize a script on how to demonstrate the copier—complete with hand motions! For some reason, we salespeople feel most comfortable when we are speaking. We feel we are in control."

If I am selling you that Z4, it is *so* much easier for me to memorize the length of the wheelbase than it is to modify each sales presentation to fit the specific needs of the individual customer.

If I'm serving coffee, it is more efficient to keep sloshing java in the cups than to offer several varieties and sophisticated blends that appeal to the varied tastes of individual customers.

And if I'm selling trailers—which I do—it is a heck of a lot quicker and less costly for me to encourage you to fit your needs into the trailers I build than it is for me to build trailers to fit your individual and specific needs.

It's just easier. And it creates one of the great disconnects between customers and business! As Ron Karr states, "The truth of the matter is, we are less in control of the relationship when we are speaking. The strength you need comes from being attentive to the answers from the questions you ask."

We will examine how this comes into play—and how to resolve this issue—in greater detail later in this chapter.

Desperation Communication

Okay, I'm certain you have never experienced this aspect of disconnection with customers. So don't get your defenses up . . . this is for other readers, not you.

You've never been so desperate to make a sale that you "hawked" your goods and services in an "ABC" manner. You've never had to make "goal" or "quota" for the month. You've never had investors or bankers or the Street looking over your shoulder for this quarter's results.

You've probably never been pushed—been desperate—like that.

But I *have.* Let me tell you from my personal experience, it makes you focus on the product instead of the customer. And the irony is, it prevents you from developing relationships with customers.

I remember the early days of my career, when the focus of my life was on professional speaking. I distinctly recall sitting in my office—

the converted guest room in a two-bedroom apartment in Columbus, Indiana—looking at my bare calendar. I needed money; therefore, I needed bookings!

Do you believe that I said to myself, *I need to find more ways to be of value to prospects and customers*? I didn't. Instead I said, *If I want to eat—I gotta book some speeches!*

Did I get on the phone and attempt to learn more about the needs and goals of prospects? NO! I started "dialing for dollars"! I just knew that if I made enough calls to enough people, then surely someone somewhere was having a meeting where they needed a speech. I tried to find some poor jerk who forgot to book a speaker and was in trouble because he was going to have a couple hundred coworkers in a breakout room at the Holiday Inn in a month, and had to have something—anything—happen after dinner.

I hate to admit it, but it's true. I only cared about their business *after* they booked me to speak to their organization. The late Earl Nightingale used to call this the "wood stove" syndrome. He said this approach made as much sense as sitting in front of a stove and saying, "Okay—if you give me some heat, *then* I will put in some wood."[2]

I've also heard this described as the "chaff" method. Today's sophisticated military has missiles that are targeted with an amazing degree of precision. They can find and destroy an enemy's aircraft even as it flies at great speed and employs maneuvers to elude the rocket. Because of this, it is easy to forget that in earlier times—such as World War II—the strategy was to fill the skies with "chaff." The enemy aircraft would run into the chaff and be damaged or destroyed.

Just like the military of olden days, instead of being precise and targeted, desperate salespeople throw huge amounts of junk into the air—and then hope a prospect will run into it.

Unfortunately, it is not just individual salespeople who resort to this approach. Desperate organizations take desperate measures—customers be damned.

The *Puget Sound Business Journal* reported on a division of the successful company Coinstar named Meals.com that was underperforming. So, in a desperate communication move, Meals.com fogged out a lengthy e-mail to three hundred thousand customers, including those who had opted out of this type of marketing! One of the results of this action was that the parent company sought ways to distance itself from Meals.com's poor performance and practices. As the newspaper accurately reports:

> This kind of damn-the-rules behavior also irrevocably erodes customer confidence that the company will do what it promises. Brands that are new are also fragile, and it doesn't take much to tear them down. The justification [such as Meals.com's] that few complained ignores the fact that most unhappy customers don't complain. They just stop doing business with a company.

In other words, we become so desperate to sell our products that we stop caring about the very people whom we want to buy them. And that's dumb. But, of course, it's never happened to you. Right?

The Key to Solving This Disconnection

The answer is *not* to simply forget about the product and focus on the customer!

The key is to have a customer focus every step of the way as it relates to your product—design and marketing, just to name a couple of points. Ask yourself: *Is there empathy* (as discussed in the previous chapter) *and a passion for the customer at all levels in my organization? Are the engineers in my company as committed to customers as the sales team?*

I know the second question may sound somewhat naive and unrealistic—but why shouldn't they? Why shouldn't the engineers who design our trailers at United Trailer be every bit as customer focused as the marketing professionals who sell those trailers? If you are Procter & Gamble, why shouldn't your chemists become as intensely committed to the homemaker who buys the Tide as they are to the formula that *is* the product?

The compliance officer who doesn't care about the people who are investing in a financial product should be fired. Without that passion, at some point he will make the wrong call. If you don't think that's true, pick up a few old issues of the *Wall Street Journal* and read about the recent scandal in the mutual fund industry.

Please don't get the wrong idea—I'm not suggesting that this kind of passion involves any outlandishly enthusiastic behavior. I mean a fervent commitment, regardless of personality style, to the customer by every employee at your organization, at every step along the way. However, notice the parallel between the viewpoint from the previous chapter—that only specific areas in an organization are responsible for customer service—and the belief that certain professionals should be more "product-centric" than "customer-centric." Notice a pattern?

Let's explore how this focus on the customer works in three areas:

1. product design

2. product manufacturing

3. service delivery

Product Design

Perhaps the leading advocate for a customer focus in product design is Tom Peters. I am not in agreement with everything Peters says about management; however, his "rantings" about product design should have great resonance in any organization.

Peters believes that products are sometimes created for the engineers who design them rather than the customer who will be using them. I think of this every time I use my cell phone. I have a wonderfully technically advanced phone in my pocket. I have two problems with it. First, it is *so* advanced that I can't figure out how to use many of the features! OK, I'm overstating. Here is the real problem—the learning curve and the time necessary to educate myself on how to use the features is so demanding that I will not invest the effort.

I'm sure it is great to have a phone that will check your e-mail, for example. Unfortunately, when I learned how to do it, I overloaded the memory of the phone, because I get so much spam that the phone couldn't handle my volume of e-mail. (I'll bet you have a similar problem.) Sure, it sounds terrific to get your e-mail on your tiny cell phone. But if you can't use it in the real world, what value is it to your customer?

My business partner, Tim Durham, is a major investor in Brightpoint, one of the largest distributors of cell phones in the world. Through Tim, I've learned some of the terminology regarding the design of these products. We're all aware of the particular type of design called a "flip phone." But did you know that the phones that do not flip—for example, most Nokia and Sony Ericsson phones—are called "candy bars"? After you hear the phrase, it makes a lot of sense—my phone is about the size, weight, and shape of a candy bar.

Another problem I have with my current phone is this: when you're used to a flip phone and then change to a candy bar, the keypad is now unprotected. In other words, what was formerly covered by the "flip" is now exposed. Imagine my embarrassment when a friend of mine on the East Coast left me a sleepy but slightly perturbed message asking me what in the heck I was doing calling him at 2:00 AM! We had, in fact, talked earlier in the evening—then I had slipped the phone back in my pocket. Now, at 11:00 PM on the West Coast (where I was), the unprotected "Send" button had somehow activated, and the phone redialed him. Knowing my number from caller ID, he answered, thinking it must be something important for me to be calling at that hour. Instead, he heard the sounds of my television broadcasting the late local news.

I realize that all I have to do on my phone is hit two simple buttons and a "keypad lock" is engaged that will prevent this type of accident. However, that's not as intuitive as just flipping the lid closed, as I did with my previous phone. To me, that's a flaw in the design from the customer's perspective. I won't be buying another.

Tom Peters uses a great example when he talks about the bottles of toiletries in a hotel room. Obviously designed by twenty-somethings with perfect eyesight, the problem is that we forty- and fifty-somethings who actually stay in the room are naked in the shower, squinting without our reading glasses, and attempting to see if we are about to put shampoo, cream rinse, or hand lotion on our follicles. No one at the hair care company stopped to think about the customer! The design of the bottle was obviously not given a great deal of care and consideration, but I'll bet anything the cost of the ingredients in that bottle have been scrutinized repeatedly.

To parallel a point mentioned in an earlier chapter, it's not what's inside the bottle; it's the person putting it in her hair that counts. Isn't it amazing that a product can be created with so much effort and diligence—only to arrive in the hands of a customer who can't even read what the heck it is!

On the other hand, companies that do it right receive great acclaim. The first product that comes to mind for me is the Apple iPod. I spend so much time on planes that I can't imagine how I got along without it. Sure, it's wonderful for music, but I listen to books, record personal voice memos, use it as my alarm clock in a hotel room, store digital photos, and back up the important data from my computer—all on this little marvel.

When Apple developed a second line—called the iPod mini, a tiny version of the original—many "critics" claimed that it was going to be a disaster for the company. At $249 it was overpriced, the reviewers proclaimed. However, Steve Jobs and crew are having the last laugh— the "mini" is a terrific success. In fact, many of the first buyers were customers who already owned a full-featured iPod and wanted another, smaller version! Is the design of your product so "insanely great" (to steal a Jobs line) that people who own your product would stand in line to sign a waiting list (as happened with the iPod mini on its release) to get a *second version of what they already own*?

Design that focuses on the customer is possible in any industry for any product. In May 2004, *Architectural Digest* published a collector's edition called "The Great Design Issue." Part of what I enjoyed most was that the magazine featured great designs in every imaginable product—not just homes. Everything from tea infusers to tables, from a chaise longue to a Cartier, from a bathtub to a Boxster. (And, of course, the aforementioned iPod was cited. It was called everything from "sleek and stylish" by one designer to "brilliant" by another.)

I would suggest that you pick up this issue of *Architectural Digest* if you have anything to do with product design in your organization. Keep it on your desk as an important reminder that amazing design both strengthens the emotional ties your customer has to your organization and your product *and* lengthens the life cycle of the product as well! We've seen hundreds of car designs, for example, come and go; yet the classics, from the Volkswagen "Beetle" to the Porsche 911, have stood the test of time. In fact, one could argue that superior design is the *only* reason that some companies—like Apple Computer—have even survived, given the hypercompetitive nature of business today.

Author Nathan Cool, in his book *The Four Keys to Successful Design* (iUniverse, November, 2003), states that the key elements to product design are also the factors in exploring human development. His keys are the following:

1. Inspiration

2. Innovation

3. Exploration

4. Creation

The book's subtitle is pretty remarkable: *A Motivational Approach from Thought to Finish.* In other words, design is about motivation. It is first having an *inspiration.* My suggestion is that you could think of customers (and their needs and wants) as the cornerstone of your inspiration. The great designs we've previously discussed were born first of an inspiration—from creating a car for the common people of a nation ("Volkswagen," roughly translated from its original German, means "car of the people") to a simple yet elegant tea infuser that makes it easy to brew loose-leaf tea of your choosing instead of depending on what is inside a prepackaged tea bag.

Then, you *innovate*—and shouldn't your innovation be one of value to the people who will actually use the product as opposed to simply doing something different? People who perform stand-up comedy for a living will tell you there is a cult-like following among comedians for a few performers that ordinary folks like you and me have never heard of. These legendary comedians are remarkably innovative, yet their material plays to *other comedians*, not the audience. Certainly they are to be commended for their innovation; however, in business, success comes through appealing to an audience that will pay for your product in one way or another.

Miller Brewing's Clear Beer was certainly innovative—and was the talk of the industry—yet not something their audience (customers) wanted to purchase. Therefore, the innovation was dropped from the marketplace.

Third, you *explore*—you build your design through exploring a number of inspired, innovative options. In his groundbreaking book on creativity, *A Whack on the Side of the Head*, author Roger von Oech states that most of our problems regarding creativity—and I would suggest this includes creative product design—come from our training as elementary-school children.[3] We were taught that there was a "right answer." For example, two plus two is *always* four. The answer to the question "Who was the sixteenth president?" is *always* Abraham Lincoln. Therefore, once we get to the answer, we stop exploring. However, in real life there is almost always *more* than one "right" answer. Yet, because of our training, humans *stop* when they reach the first "right" answer—never exploring for more, and better, ideas. The key to creativity is to keep exploring!

The fourth key is *creation*. Another word that could be applied here is *execution*. Designs—and creative, innovative ideas—that remain undeveloped on the drawing board are pretty useless. Only those ideas we place into action have traction with customers.

As I have gone through the process of researching and writing this book, I have been told by numerous people that they have "no idea how someone could write a book." The very thought of it seems so overwhelming to most professionals, I guess. Part of the reason Nathan Cool's ideas regarding product design struck me must be (in some part) because I saw a real connection with writing a book. You have to be inspired by something—in my case, it is the disconnection between organizations and their customers. You need to be innovative in your approach—and to expand that innovation and enhance it . . . through the exploration of alternative ideas, applications, and philosophies.

However, I've met so many would-be authors who miss out on the fourth point, creation. The inspiration, innovation, and exploration have little value unless you put the seat of your pants into the seat of the chair and write it out. Only through the actual creation of the book (or product or service) do your ideas, designs, and concepts have any chance of reaching and resonating with the customer. As I write this, I realize that these ideas of mine may—or may not—achieve success in the marketplace of business books. However (as corny and trite as this may sound), I also know that these ideas have *zero* chance unless I create the book. The same principle works for your product or service, no matter what the specifics are.

By the way, the best advice on writing I've ever received was from motivational speaker Zig Ziglar, who told me that he had "never written a book." I looked at him as though he must be losing his mind. "Zig," I said, "I own several of the books you've written. What do you mean?"

"Well, Scott," he replied in his trademark slow Mississippi drawl, "it is much too daunting a task to write a book. What I have done is to break it down and write chapters. I would write five or so pages a day until I had a chapter. Then I would start on another chapter and write five pages a day, and so on. And, do you know what? After I had ten or twelve of those chapters done, some people told me that I had written a *book*." Zig's smile said it all: the key to creation is to break down every project into small, achievable tasks.

> The key to creation is to break down every project into small, achievable tasks.

Go back and look at your product design—is it customer focused? Or are you like the comedian, playing consciously or subconsciously to your peers and colleagues, and then wondering why you aren't connecting with a larger audience?

The point to all of this is, of course, that no matter what your product is, you *can* design it to be compelling and amazing for your customers.

Product Manufacturing

After the goods or services have been designed, you have to continue with a heightened sense of customer sensitivity to manufacture and distribute your product in a manner that eliminates the disconnection so common in today's business world.

At Champion Trailers near Dallas, Texas—a company owned by the privately held part of our company—we build very sophisticated trailers for many applications, but most notably for racing teams in NASCAR and the Indy Racing League (IRL). We have been the dominant player in the IRL for several years; however, we longed for business in NASCAR. As you're probably aware, auto racing has become America's number one spectator sport. Yet open-wheel racing, like that of the IRL and their flagship race, the Indianapolis 500, has declined somewhat in popularity. On the other hand, stock car racing—NASCAR—has grown exponentially in race attendance, television viewership, sales of licensed goods, and just about every other measurement one could apply.

When we landed our first major deal in NASCAR for the Dodge Team, led by racing genius Ray Everham, we were naturally thrilled. We wanted to manufacture the most visually exciting—as well as functional—racing trailer on the NASCAR circuit. So we went all out—except too much of our focus was on building the best *trailer* . . . *instead* of the best solution for our *customer*. I know I have a high degree of prejudice, but I believe we built an unbelievably beautiful, amazing trailer. It was remarkable in its appearance—especially with all of the chrome that we had placed all over the trailer so it would be distinguished visually in a dramatic way from our competition.

Imagine our pride when we showed it to our customers! Imagine our disappointment when they looked at us and said, "Chrome? Are you *kidding?*"

We forgot one little thing: to stay attractive, chrome must be clean . . . which means it must be polished and maintained. The schedules of NASCAR teams and crews are so demanding that they are border-line ridiculous. It is not only the actual racing that creates such a time crunch; these teams also have to deal with qualifying, testing, sponsor events, promotional appearances, travel, and much more. There is hardly enough time to get the trailer to the track, much less keep an inordinate amount of chrome polished so that the trailer looks great for sponsors and fans.

By striving to manufacture an amazing product, we had practically created a product our customer couldn't use.

Fortunately for us, we had not just built a trailer—we had created a relationship. Our communication and bond were strong enough with the Everham team that they felt open to giving us feedback and allowing us to continue working to manufacture exactly what they wanted. If the relationship had not been there, they could've easily gone to our major competitor. Because they knew we were truly committed to creating a compelling experience for our customer, we were able to save the project—and the business.

The problem for many businesses, of course, is that they never get the chance to work on an intensely personal basis with their customers. If you're Schick, for example, trying to improve your market share against a competitor holding 80 percent of the market—like Gillette—you just don't get the chance to deal with each of your customers in the manner in which we worked with the Dodge racing team of Ray Everham.

Because of this, most organizations become so "product myopic" that they design, package, and manufacture the product the way the organization wants it—instead of the way the customer desires. In the bygone era when Henry Ford could state, "A customer can have any color car they want—as long as it's black," that philosophy could work. Today—in a time when you can call Dell and they will custom-manufacture a computer for you—the product-centric approach won't cut it with customers.

In their 1999 book, *Mass Customization,* authors Stan Davis and

Joseph Pine pioneered the idea that it is possible to manufacture products and services to a mass audience, yet still make them customized to the needs of specific customers.

As Dallas Fed Chief Economist Dr. W. Michael Cox wrote:

> Americans have always preferred customized products, but they couldn't always afford them. Now, companies are finding ways to deliver exactly what we want at prices competitive with those of mass production. Information Age technology—primarily the computer—has erased yesterday's edict that customization must carry a high price. "Mass customization" offers a consumer the best of both worlds. It embodies the good qualities from the era of hand production—custom design and individualized service. And it retains the most significant gain from the era of mass production—low cost.[4]

It's important to note that Davis and Pine did not suggest in their book that "mass customization" was solely a manufacturing process. It is *a total business philosophy* that must be executed in all segments of the organization.

As *Fortune* magazine stated in an article on the subject:

> Computer-controlled factory equipment and industrial robots make it easier to quickly readjust assembly lines. The proliferation of bar-code scanners makes it possible to track virtually every part and product. Databases now store trillions of bytes of information, including individual customers' predilections for everything from cottage cheese to suede boots. Digital printers make it a cinch to change product packaging on the fly. Logistics and supply-chain management software tightly coordinates manufacturing and distribution.[5]

In other words, as Joseph Pine says, "Anything you can digitize, you can customize."

In their article, "Customizing Customization," Joseph Lampel and Henry Mintzberg stated that there are five variations of this customization:

1. *Pure standardization* is the conventional assembly-line manufacturing of identical items using standard parts and uniform assembly procedures. Products are engineered to attract the greatest volume of customers. These buyers have no impact on design, production, or distribution. Examples include Henry Ford's Model T automobiles, pencils, and paper clips.

2. *Segmented standardization* produces a basic product with a few distinctions that are targeted to the preferences of a particular group of customers. The number of options increases, and manufacturers may customize distribution, but purchasers still do not have any direct impact on product design or production. Examples cited in the report include such items as bread (whole wheat, white, and rye) and shoes (high heels, flats, and mid-heel styles).

3. *Customized standardization* makes products to order out of a fixed group of mass-produced components. The choices are sometimes limited to adding components to a basic unit. Buyers, therefore, may affect how the product is assembled and distributed; however, they do not impact the design and production of those parts. The example cited in the report is the process of buying a car: customers may choose paint and upholstery and select optional equipment to add to a uniform chassis and body design.

4. *Tailored customization* takes it to the next level. At this stage, the process allows the customer to customize items such as the fabrication, assembly, and distribution. The manufacturer retains authority over the design—offering the buyer various options, such as choice from different kinds of materials. Depending on the specific product, the manufacturer sometimes offers to modify the design to meet the customer's needs. Common examples of tailored customization include purchasing a tailor-made suit instead of one "off the rack"—and selecting and printing wedding invitations.

5. *Pure customization* represents the opposite end of the continuum from purely standardized products. Pure customized products or services are those that are "made to order" in every aspect of design, fabrication, assembly, and distribution. Pure customization

mandates that the buyer and seller collaborate in developing the product or service. The example cited in the report is the relationship between an architect and a homeowner when designing and constructing a custom home.[6]

The important point here is that there are many organizations that do no customization—or are in the "Segmented Customization" stage—who are not there by choice. These companies are just continuing to do what they have always done. How can you redefine your product so the concentration changes at every stage—especially the manufacturing—so that your focus shifts from the product to the customer? Review each of the aforementioned stages—then ask yourself how you can take the steps to simply move to the next stage. It would be a great start.

Service Delivery

I'm sitting in front of the television watching my favorite sports team, the Indiana Pacers. The game is exciting, and I don't want to move from this spot—yet I'm getting hungrier by the moment. So I pick up the phone during a time-out and dial my local Pizza Hut. The telephone rings once, and a friendly voice answers, saying, "Thank you for calling Pizza Hut. Would the McKain household like the usual large sausage and pepperoni with thin 'n crispy crust?"

I simply respond, "You bet. Thanks!"

"You're welcome, Mr. McKain. We'll have it there for you in about thirty minutes." I smile, hang up, and get back to the game.

As mentioned previously, if you can digitize it, you can customize it. Pizza Hut knew it was the McKain house calling because of caller ID. The Pizza Hut computer kicked up info about the specific pizza ingredients we normally order. The entire process lasted less than thirty seconds—and the delivery required less than thirty minutes.

However, notice that a significant portion of the pleasure of the communication wasn't simply that the Pizza Hut product-ordering technology worked to perfection. The person answering the phone not only noticed who was placing the call, but used my name in the conversation. In other words, it is not just possessing the information—my name and product preference. The key is to use that knowledge to enhance the personalization of the transaction!

In an article in *Harvard Business Review,* James Gilmore and Joseph Pine demonstrate how hotelier Ritz-Carlton applies this approach:

> For example, to avoid annoying customers with an endless barrage of surveys on preferences, Ritz-Carlton established a less intrusive means of learning about individual needs. It observes the preferences that individual guests manifest during each stay—preferences for, say, hypoallergenic pillows, classical radio stations, or chocolate chip cookies. The company then stores that information in a database and uses it to tailor the service that each customer receives on his or her next visit. The more someone stays in Ritz-Carlton hotels, the more the company learns, and the more customized goods and services it fits into the standard Ritz-Carlton room—increasing the guest's preference for that hotel over others.[7]

For goodness' sake, who wouldn't want to stay in a hotel where they know your preferences with that degree of precision? So, when it comes to the delivery of a service experience that is externally focused on your customer instead of internally centered on your organization, how do you get from where you are to the desired point? Mariann McDonagh, vice president of global marketing for Verint Systems, in an article written for the January 2004 issue of *Customer Interaction Solutions,* provides a terrific road map through her four keys for strategically building exceptional service delivery:

1. Evaluate your current customer experience.

2. First things first: Make it predictable.

3. Step it up: Build momentum.

4. It's all about the details.

First—to get to where you want to go, you first have to know where you are. You cannot do that without a critical evaluation of your current situation. A vital question McDonagh says must be confronted is, "Is service *random* (the customer experience is left to chance) when it should be *intentional* (customer experience is meticulously planned)?" If the level of personalization your service delivery attains is based on the luck of the draw—in other words, dependent merely on the *chance* that the customer happens to encounter someone in your organization who is driven to providing personal service experiences (my other BMW salesman) as opposed to reciting product or service features (my other BMW salesman)—then your organization will have an exceedingly difficult time attaining a consistently higher level of customer loyalty.

Second—after this evaluation, strive to remove any aspect of "randomness." As McDonagh says, "Enable your . . . management to develop a customer-centric philosophy and communicate a basic strategy in terms of performance targets and quality standards. The same team should focus on your people, developing performance objectives . . . that broadly correlate to the outlined strategy. Make sure your [employees] understand the new plan and are rewarded accordingly as they work for the success of the enterprise."

Third—develop and capture momentum. The *World English Dictionary* defines *momentum* as "the power to increase or develop at an ever-growing pace." That's exactly what you need to be doing to enhance the personalization of your delivery of services: developing the strategies necessary and increasing their systematic application at an ever-growing pace. McDonagh states, "Now focus on [what the] customer measures—outcomes . . . loyalty. Your technology is already in place, so now is the time to be sure you are using it wisely to provide measurement tools for analyzing customer behavior and the extent to which your organization is meeting *their* needs." Notice that McDonagh is basing all measurement on customer *outcomes*—not merely on actions that lend themselves to convenient measurement.

Fourth—as the old cliché goes, "The devil is in the details." Here's what McDonagh says: "Your . . . philosophy is now further extended to tailor service propositions by individual or customer segments, and ser-vice is a brand promise that you keep. You invest significantly in training, coaching, performance management and communications. These elements [will] make motivation intrinsic within your organization."

John Graham, in an article for *The American Salesman*, described the importance of sweating the small stuff:

> Our daughter was conducting a campus tour at Boston University of prospective students and their parents, when the Chancellor, Dr. John Silber, joined the group. "Why did he take his time to do that?" she asked. There may be a number of reasons, but it suggested to me that the head of the nation's fifth largest private university understands the value of taking care of the details. Everything is important in getting to the goal. If we skip taking care of the little things, we'll be faced with dealing with the big problems.[8]

As a friend told me recently, "I hate the title of that book *Don't Sweat the Small Stuff!* If you don't sweat the small stuff, then the small stuff becomes big, big stuff!"

Putting It All Together

As David Whitwam, the highly successful and recently retired CEO of Whirlpool, said in an interview with the *Harvard Business Review* in 1994, "We have to provide a compelling reason other than price for consumers to buy Whirlpool-built products. We can do that only by understanding the consumer better than anyone else does and then translating our understanding into clearly superior product designs, features, and after-sales support."[9]

If you don't sweat the small stuff, then the small stuff becomes big, big stuff!

No matter what your organization does, examine where your focus is maintained. If it is on your products, you run the risk of alienating your most valuable attribute, your customers. This may be a highly uncomfortable process for you and your organization. When all of your training, time, and effort have centered on the design, manufacturing, and servicing of your product, to suggest that now you need to move your focus externally sounds like sacrilege. However, if you do not change your focus, your customers may change their supplier.

Executive Summary

The Second Disconnection is that what customers REALLY want is for you to focus upon their unique needs, wants, challenges, and situations— yet most organizations focus upon their own products and services.

- Organizations focus upon their own products and services— instead of having a focus upon their customers—for two basic, simple reasons:
  - *It's easier.*
    - It's easier to respond with memorized facts and figures about the product or services that we have worked so hard to engineer, manufacture, market, and distribute than it is to learn about your problem and create a tailored solution for your unique benefit.
    - By concentrating on our product and/or service, we have the mistaken belief that we are in control of the marketing/sales process . . . not realizing that if we do not know the needs and desires of our customers we ultimately cannot respond to them.
  - *We're desperate.*
    - Often we need to stimulate sales quickly—therefore, we don't want to take the time necessary to build relationships and craft unique solutions. So, we start aggressively pushing sales—sometimes at the expense of customer relationships.

- There are three basic arenas in which we can bridge the gap between the personal focus that customers REALLY want and the product or service focus that organizations often deliver:

  ○ *Product design*

    - We need to understand that by focusing upon—then creating and executing—amazing product design, organizations can expand the lifecycle of their products and create a compelling experience for customers.

    - Reevaluate all products and services to ensure they truly meet the needs of your customers in today's environment.

      - Sure, the product works—but can your customers read the label? Is there an "ease of use" engineered into the product and its packaging?

    - Understand there are four major elements to compelling product design:

      1. *Inspiration:* Is the product or service compelling, unique, and inspired?

      2. *Innovation:* Is there an innovative, fresh aspect that will provide a competitive differentiation for your product or service?

      3. *Exploration:* Don't stop at the "first right answer." Constantly explore additional ways to improve the product—and to expand its audience.

      4. *Creation:* It is not enough to have compelling product or service design. That design must be created . . . it must find execution in the real world. Great design without implementation benefits neither the organization nor its customers or prospects.

  ○ *Product manufacturing*

    - This is the age of "mass customization." Anything that can be digitized—as we find so frequently in today's world—can be customized.

- Customization has five levels:
  1. Pure standardization
     - For example: the "Model T" Ford, pencils, paper clips
  2. Segmented standardization
     - Bread (choose whole wheat, white, rye, etc.); women's shoes (high heels, flats, midheel)
  3. Customized standardization
     - Paint and upholstery chosen for your automobile; optional equipment to add to a computer built for you
  4. Tailored customization
     - A suit tailored for you instead of "off the rack"; personalized wedding invitations
  5. Pure customization
     - An architect's design and the contractor's work in the custom building of a home

The higher the level of customization, the more emotional impact the product or service has on the customer.

- *Service delivery*
  - Organizations should use the tools of technology to create customized—and highly personalized—service for their customers.
  - There are four steps to personalizing service:
    1. *Evaluate your current customer experience:* How engaged are customers with your organization?
    2. *Make it predictable:* Can your customers rely upon your organization to consistently deliver the experiences they desire? If not, how can you make it more predictable and reliable?

3. *Step it up . . . build momentum:* Is there an increasing sense of excitement about doing business with your organization? Are you building momentum . . . not only in the marketplace, but in the minds and hearts of every customer and prospect about your company?

4. *It's all about the details:* In other words, sweat the small stuff. If you don't, the small stuff has a way of becoming big stuff—not only for your customers, but for your organization, as well.

Bridge Building
Moving from a Product Focus to a Personal Focus

- What is the approximate ratio between the time you spend educating your people on products and the time they spend learning techniques for building relationships?

- What would you estimate to be the amount of time your sales professionals (or *you!*) spend listening to customers versus talking to customers? How would your sales professionals answer that question? Is there a disconnection?

  - If you have the courage to find the answer to this question, here's where you could score huge bonus points: How would your *customers* answer that question? Are you guessing, or have you *asked* them?

    - And, if you are only guessing or assuming, what does that say about the amount of time and diligence spent on listening to customers?

- Do you have contests for employees to test their product knowledge?

  - Do you test their knowledge of customers and the customers' needs with the same intensity?

- Does your product or service have an amazing and compelling design? If not, outline the specific steps you have to take to get there.

- What level of standardization/customization do your products and services have? Is that by your design or just happenstance?

- When you deliver your service to the customer, do you really (and I mean REALLY) get the details right?

- What specific steps do you take to prove to your clients that you care more about *them* than you do their business?

3

THE THIRD DISCONNECTION

What Customers REALLY Want: *Reciprocal Loyalty*
What Business Supplies: *Endless Prospecting*

Pick up a newspaper—and I mean *any* newspaper—and I'm willing to bet that you will easily find an advertisement attempting to recruit you to a particular brand of wireless telephone service. It seems as if these phone companies are constantly, relentlessly, endlessly prospecting to find more customers for their service.

So, have you ever wondered why these companies don't spend a little less on advertising and a little more on improving the quality of the services they provide existing customers? Does it irritate you just a bit to see all of these ads for "buy one, get one free" phones, when you had to pay for every cell phone for everyone in your family? Do the "introductory offers" of a million minutes for ten bucks bother you when you aren't able to get the same rate from a company that you've been doing business with for years?

If you were agreeing with any of these questions, congratulations. You've experienced the Third Disconnection.

Customers *want* to be loyal. They desire (more than they can express) to have the feeling when they walk into your business that Norm had when he entered the bar in *Cheers*. Yet, it seems as if the majority of companies are doing everything they can to prevent customers from being the consistently connected consumers that every organization needs. Nowhere is this disconnection more "in the face" of customers than the area of "loyalty vs. prospecting."

When you consider a study (published in the *Harvard Business Review* in the March 1, 1996, issue) that found most companies lose *half their customers* in a five-year period, you can see that this disconnection has a profound impact on the financial success of your business.

And to continue the mobile phone company rant, doing research on whether or not people like their wireless companies seems to me akin to asking whether or not teenagers like homework. Yet that's exactly what the University of Michigan has done. According to their customer satisfaction index, mobile phone service beat only cable television providers as the industry least able to create positive experiences for their customers. You should find it more than just an interesting coincidence that the industry cited as the one doing the most prospecting for new customers is also at the bottom of the pile in creating the experiences that generate customer loyalty.

So, how did the representatives of the mobile phone companies respond to this study?

Well . . . as you might imagine from an industry so lowly regarded by its customers, they once again proved that they just don't get it.

Eric Rabe, a spokesman for Verizon Communications said—ready for this?—"Compared to what? Lands' End? You have to compare apples to apples. I wouldn't compare the customer experience of dealing with a complicated technology with buying a shirt. It's just a whole different challenge."

Sorry, Mr. Rabe, but your answer stinks. The pattern of thinking that you've just displayed is what's wrong with mobile phone service—and almost all customer experiences—in America. You say that your organization is in an industry that involves "complicated technology," yet there are many businesses in other industries that must also deal with your challenge of coping with complexity and somehow find a way to maintain extraordinarily high standards.

For example, I would presume that operating an airline is a pretty tough challenge, but jetBlue not only meets our expectations—it exceeds them. My guess is that manufacturing cutting-edge electronic equipment and distributing it on a worldwide basis is no walk in the park, but a lot of us are thrilled with Sony's highly advanced products. Please note that Sony doesn't ask me to care about their technical challenges. jetBlue has yet to request that I have sympathy for the complexity of airline management. You're telling me—your customer—that I'm supposed to care about how tough *your* challenge is? I don't. That's *your* job.

As customers, we have a right to expect you to do your job. We have a right to expect that the service will work the way you promise, that our bill will be correct, that we will be dealt with properly and with empathy when we have a problem. And we hope that you are professional and visionary enough to understand that if you want a loyal customer, you have to find a way to create some kind of compelling experience for me as I do business with your organization.

And until you do, we're going to continue to believe that your commitment to your customers is minuscule. We're going to continue to believe that the way your industry operates pretty much sucks. We're not going to give you a pass because you can't do your job. Get your act together.

Can you hear me now?

(End of my mobile phone company rant—and, believe it or not, I see some positive trends in this industry beginning to appear. You'll read more about them later in this chapter.)

Sales and Sales Training

Interestingly, when Alec Baldwin gave the advice to "always be closing" in the aforementioned movie, *Glengarry Glen Ross*, he was giving a speech about an incentive program—where the award was obtaining high-quality leads for the winning salesperson to prospect. When I first went to sales training classes, I was taught that you "can't be closing unless you've already been prospecting." Maybe you were taught (as I was) that "sales is a numbers game." In other words, the more you prospect, the greater the likelihood that you'll make more sales. Therefore, cold calling was an essential function of any business.

I took the bait and started making cold prospecting calls—from a script that sounded something like this:

"Hello, Mr. Smith. My name is Scott McKain, and I represent the XYZ Company. How are you today? [Pause briefly for a mumbled response from prospect.] Great. Glad to hear it. Mr. Smith, my company has assisted other businesses to grow their profits. Does that sound interesting to you?"

Could that be any more manipulative? Could it be any less client focused? Is this any way to begin to build a relationship? Of course not.

I even attended programs on developing strategies for "overcoming cold-call reluctance." I learned about the "third-party endorsement" and the "feel, felt, found" method—the one where you say, "I understand how you *feel*. A lot of people *felt* that way until they *found* out about [insert product feature here]."

It was amazing how many tricks were presented! At one seminar, the speaker put a list on the flip chart. It read as follows:

- Overcoming the gatekeeper
- Overcoming common objections
  - I'm too busy.
  - I'm happy with what I have.
  - It costs too much.
  - I'm not interested.
  - I want to see some literature.
  - I don't make the decision.
  - I'm the wrong person to talk to.
  - NO!
- Overcoming call reluctance
- Overcoming prospect indecision

I sat there and looked at this list and understood one very important thing about the seminar I was about to hear: my interaction with the prospect was a function of my *overcoming* her! In other words, the way to begin my relationship with a customer was to conquer what she was thinking and defeat her feelings! When a relationship begins with one party attempting to vanquish the other, what are the chances of long-term, reciprocal loyalty?

In sales training, we were taught that successfully applying these tricks and techniques in our interaction with the prospect would lead us to a profitable consummation of the sale—in a process called the "close." If you have any belief that words do have meaning, then you must examine how our psychology of business and of selling has been impacted by that little word . . . *close.*

A good sales professional is often called a "strong closer." One Web site on sales (ChangingMinds.org) lists these closing techniques:

- 1-2-3 Close—close with the principle of three.
- Affordable Close—ensuring people can afford what you are selling.
- Alternative Close—offering a limited set of choices.
- Assumptive Close—acting as if they are ready to decide.
- Balance-sheet Close—adding up the pros and the cons.
- Best-time Close—emphasize how now is the best time to buy.
- Bonus Close—offer delighter to clinch the deal.
- Bracket Close—make three offers—with the target in the middle.
- Calendar Close—put it in the diary.
- Companion Close—sell to the person with them.
- Compliment Close—flatter them into submission.
- Concession Close—give them a concession in exchange for the close.
- Conditional Close—link closure to resolving objections.
- Courtship Close—woo them to the close.
- Demonstration Close—show them the goods.

- Doubt Close—show you doubt the product and let them disagree.
- Economic Close—help them pay less for what they get.
- Embarrassment Close—make *not* buying embarrassing.
- Emotion Close—trigger identified emotions.
- Empathy Close—empathize with them, and then sell to your new friend.
- Empty-offer Close—make them an empty offer that the sale fills.
- Future Close—close on a future date.
- Golden Bridge Close—make the only option attractive.
- Humor Close—relax them with humor.
- IQ Close—say how this is for intelligent people.
- Never-the-best-time Close—for customers who are delaying.
- No-hassle Close—make it as easy as possible.
- Now-or-never Close—to hurry things up.
- Ownership Close—act as if they own what you are selling.
- Price-promise Close—promise to meet any other price.
- Puppy Close—acting cute to invoke sympathy and a nurturing response.
- Quality Close—sell on quality, not on price.
- Repetition Close—repeat a closing action several times.
- Retrial Close—go back to square one.
- Reversal Close—act as if you do not want them to buy the product.
- Selective-deafness Close—respond only to what you want to hear.

(used by permission)

The reason I wanted you to see all of these closes is to understand something very important—there is an overwhelming number of techniques being taught by organizations that can be very helpful in making a sale . . . and destructive in building a *relationship* . . . which is, of course, what customers REALLY want.

To Make It Personal . . .

Take these exact closing techniques—but this time, transpose them to a personal situation instead of a professional one. What if your boyfriend got down on one knee, pulled what appeared to be a box about the size of an engagement ring from his pocket, looked up into your eyes . . . and tried the "Reversal Close"? ("You probably don't want this, do you?") How about the "Conditional Close"? ("If I can overcome your objections regarding my horrible drinking habits, will you spend the rest of your life with me?") Consider the "Quality Close" ("You won't find anyone better than me"). Any woman would be horrified—and rightfully so!

The first time the subject of marriage was brought up between my now-wife and me, I'm thankful that she didn't attempt to "close the deal." If she would've attempted the "Calendar Close"—"Well, since you've brought up marriage, how does November 20 look for you?"— I would've dashed away!

Relationships aren't subject to "closing"! If you examine most personal relationships, you discover that a "closing" means the relationship is ending—not beginning. When a relationship ends badly, or if there is a death, or abuse in the relationship, for example, we seek "closure" . . . to discover a sense of finality and resolve our feelings.

In a true relationship there is a *reciprocal loyalty.* You count on your spouse to be faithful, and he or she expects the same from you. You depend on friends and family to provide emotional support when you need it—and you stand ready to do the same for them.

The Josephson Institute of Ethics states that there are "six pillars of character" in making ethical choices and building lasting relationships:

1. Trustworthiness
2. Respect
3. Responsibility
4. Fairness

5. Caring

6. Citizenship[1]

The institute states that a hallmark of trustworthiness is someone who understands the importance of loyalty and appreciates that it is a higher calling than merely "looking out for others."

You cannot be loyal to a group or an individual—and display the other "pillars of character" such as "caring" and "respect"—if you do not have *their* best interests at heart. People understand this principle innately and somehow just "know" when you do not have genuine concern for their needs and wants. Somewhere along the way we learn that endless prospecting means (from the customer's perspective) you're more concerned about selling more of your stuff than helping our situation.

Yet countless organizations run through the cycle of endless prospecting and even spend significant amounts of money to train their people to learn these tricks and techniques, then wonder why so many of their clients are bolting for the door.

Front Door—Back Door

Prospecting is really the attempt by business to attract new customers, isn't it? Every organization wants to expand its client base and grow the business. Obviously there is nothing wrong with that—in fact, it is mandatory. Your company *needs* to have your front door open—in other words, to take the steps to bring new customers inside!

The problem, however, is that many companies fail to examine two important points:

1. How do the methods of customer acquisition set the tone for the experience that they will expect once they pass through the "front door"?

2. What *happens* to these customers once they are inside?

To put it another way, many organizations have the front door open, but are using tricks and techniques to get customers to come inside instead of forming (through their corporate culture and their actions) the foundation of a loyal, long-term customer relationship.

And organizations have been focusing so much on the front door, they haven't noticed that the back door is wide open—and customers are streaming out!

Here's an obvious point, but one that, for some reason, so many organizations seem to be missing: *it doesn't matter how many new customers you are bringing in the front, if you're losing more out the back!*

In my first book, I discussed how all organizations have a "recruitment" strategy for finding new employees, but significantly fewer have a "retention" strategy for keeping and growing the employees they've brought on board. Now I'm suggesting to you that the *same* principle applies to the manner in which many businesses deal with customers!

You don't have to look far to find it—go back to that newspaper we were discussing at the beginning of the chapter. When you think about it, the only thing any advertisement really represents is an *invitation* to go through the sponsor's front door. You'll see countless ads from businesses wanting you, the prospect, to come inside. These same companies often have not a clue how to develop the *experiences* that engender loyalty with the customer they've just acquired. It's like the old line about the dog chasing cars—he wouldn't know what to do if he ever caught one!

It doesn't matter how many new customers you are bringing in the front, if you're losing more out the back!

Yet because many businesses will center their activities on acquisition instead of retention—on prospecting instead of loyalty—they create a huge disconnect between what customers really want and what the organization is providing.

Customer Interaction Breeds Customer Loyalty

What is customer loyalty, anyway? Certainly you can state the easy answer—the customer keeps coming back. However, that doesn't seem to really get at the heart of what engenders true, *lasting* loyalty. As Richard Morrison, president of U.S. Operations of Respond, Inc., wrote in the October 2001 issue of *Customer Interaction Solutions*, "Ask 50 companies how to define customer loyalty and what they are doing to achieve it, and undoubtedly, just as many responses will be given."

In the May 2000 issue of the *Journal of Advertising Research*, Scott Bailey of Targetbase, an Omnicom Group company, advances the point that "Customer loyalty only occurs when the two parties perceive that the relationship between them is equal."

Back to Morrison:

> By consistently responding to and acting on their feedback, true value is created in the eyes of customers, resulting in very satisfied and truly loyal customers who repeat business with the organization and refer others with passion. Furthermore, when the loyalty process extends across the enterprise—to every customer touch point, from the reception desk to senior-level executives—companies glean more insight into what customers value and how the company can better meet their needs—for life.

I would suggest that a portion of the disconnection in the area of customer loyalty stems from the error many businesses make in ascertaining the depth of their relationship with the customer.

To use the romantic analogy again, consider the situation between two people when they are dating. If they are both "just dating"—and they each understand the other—they are comfortable in the relationship. If they are both "serious" about the other—and both have the same level of commitment—they, too, are comfortable in the relationship. However, if one is "just dating" while the other is "serious" . . . well, now you have a problem.

If your customer is "serious" about building a relationship with a supplier or vendor—and through your actions of endless prospecting and a focus on your product rather than their problem you appear to be "just dating"—you have a relationship problem.

Several authors and speakers use the "Six Stages of Customer Interaction"—some call it the "Stages of a Customer's Life Cycle"— to make the point of knowing the level of intensity of your customer interaction. I first heard this approach from the legendary professional speaker Don Hutson of Memphis. The six stages are:

1. Suspect
2. Prospect
3. First-time buyer
4. Repeat customer
5. Client
6. Advocate

A "suspect" is someone who may need what you have to offer. Neither you nor he is certain—and won't be until information is shared.

A "prospect" is someone who has both the ability to purchase and the need. However, she will not do business with you until you have proved your ability to solve her problem.

A "first-time buyer" is someone who has done exactly that: purchased your product or service for the first time. He is giving you the opportunity to serve him—and is evaluating how you respond to his needs. The "grade" he gives you will determine if he takes the next step.

The "repeat customer" is obviously a former "first-time buyer" who is coming back for more. Your organization can do much to move the first-timers into the repeat category. How you execute service and product strategies—as well as how you continue to nurse the relationship along—creates repeat customers. For example, part of the reason automobile dealers want you to return to the dealership for service is to build you into a repeat customer—not just for service, but for your next car as well. The more the customer repeats the purchase process in the service department, the greater the likelihood that she will buy her next car from that dealership. (Unless, of course, the service department soils the relationship that the sales department has built!)

The term *client* suggests a deeper level of involvement by your customer—to the point that a higher level of intensity and some level of exclusivity are implied. A client isn't just shopping for the next best deal—he feels there is a reciprocal relationship that has been built and can continue to grow.

Finally, the "advocate" is the highest level of customer interaction and loyalty. These rare people are so engaged that they become promoters of your business for you. One of the definitions of the word *advocate* is "somebody who acts or intercedes on behalf of another." Ken Blanchard, of *One Minute Manager* fame, had another best seller called *Raving Fans*. In this book he suggested that the focus of your business should be to develop the highest levels of client involvement—in other words, focus on creating those advocates who become your raving fans.

The problem for many companies is that they become so focused on the acquisition of new "first-time buyers" that they inadvertently treat "clients" like "repeat customers." (They are treated without the level of personalization and emotional involvement necessary to take the relationship to a higher level.) When this happens, you fail to move "clients" into "advocates"—therefore, your "clients" instead move down the scale and start behaving as "repeat customers" and become "in play." They are now also viable "prospects" for your competition.

Also, consider this: What organization has been wildly successful without raving fans? I can't think of *any*.

The Value of Customer Loyalty

If the habitual approach of your organization is the prospecting mode, you may not yet be convinced that nothing—*nothing*—is more important to your business than customer loyalty.

I understand that it is difficult, in part because it requires a different set of skills in an area in which few of us are educated. Loyalty happens only when a relationship is present—and many managers perceive that to be a "soft" skill.

Carole Nicolaides, president of the coaching and training company Executive Leadership, wrote:

> The western civilization and our traditional management theories tend to lead us in the direction of individualistic promotion. They display our strengths rather than the demonstration of our humanness. Unfortunately, most graduate schools don't teach you how to cultivate your soft skills. A professor will give you good grades once you know XYZ, but he or she will not increase your grade for being able to deal with a difficult situation, showing compassion, or solving an unexpected problem. Yet most compliments that you or your employees receive deal more with the use of soft skills than with your actual knowledge about a particular situation. The use of these skills is what elevates your organization above the competition.[2]

Dr. Theresa E. Kane, executive director of The Academy of Professional Skills Development, put it this way in "Jobfind" in an article on September 21, 2003:

> For too many, these (soft) skills are dismissed as unimportant or expendable or they are simply taken for granted. What top performers, employers of choice and organization researchers know, however, is that these basic skills are actually more important to employers and their long-term success than work-specific technical skills. These skills are not easy; the soft stuff is hard. Trusting relationships take time to build and can be destroyed by a single violation. While most companies and job seekers don't hesitate to upgrade technical expertise, the majority let these soft skills go unchecked and neglected.

Are you and your organization investing as much in upgrading the skills that create a customer experience as you are in enhancing technical expertise?

For most companies, the answer is a resounding "No!" Yet the techniques that create loyalty have a profound impact on the profitability of your company. Remember the earlier statistic that most companies lose 50 percent of their customers within a five-year period? Consider for a moment what would happen if you would just retain a small percentage—let's say 5 percent—of those customers that you were going to lose. What would that mean to your organization?

Frederick Reichheld, author of two books on customer loyalty, states on his Web site (www.LoyaltyRules.com) that the retention of a mere 5 percent of those customers you were going to lose creates "an increase in the value of an average customer by 25 to 100%." He states that the same 5 percent improvement in retention improves profitability by the same range of 25 to 100 percent.

Reichheld continues, "This is how MBNA discovered that a 5% increase in retention lifts per-customer profit by more than 125%. This is how State Farm Insurance determined that a *1% increase* in retention will increase its capital surplus by more than *one billion dollars* over time" (emphasis added).

> Trusting relationships take time to build and can be destroyed by a single violation.

(If I were still performing from my old cold-call prospecting script, this is the point where I would insert the question "Does this sound interesting to you?")

Reichheld, director emeritus of Bain & Company and perhaps the nation's leading expert in the field of customer loyalty, proposes a six-point plan to build the "raving fans" that will create these powerful results for your organization:

1. Play to win/win.
2. Be picky.
3. Keep it simple.

4. Reward the right results.

5. Listen hard and talk straight.

6. Preach what you practice.

Play to Win/Win

Notice the contradiction between this approach and the "over-coming" approach of the sales training I received? Loyalty cannot and will not be created when you try to finish first in a battle with your customers. Just as the old cliché says, "You can win the battle and lose the war," in business we can win the sale and lose the customer. Reevaluate how your organization is approaching those "suspects" and "prospects" we discussed earlier, and determine if they feel involvement with your business is a "win-win" for them.

One approach is to reevaluate previous procedures and ascertain if there is a way to reposition them to achieve the "win-win." In the music business, for example, "fan clubs" of the recording artists were once considered a very low priority. Now, however, many artists find that by rethinking the fan club, they are better able to stay in touch with their (literally, in some cases) "raving fans"—while increasing revenue.

With the advent of the Internet, artists can now stay in constant touch with their fans and use the club as a method of preselling new recordings and concert tickets—as well as merchandise such as T-shirts.

However, the fans win as well—they feel much more connected with the artists they adore. And according to an article in *Billboard* magazine:

> With top artists reserving as much as 10% of the house in any given venue for fan-club distribution—often the best seats available—fans have motivation enough to pony up the membership fees. Musictoday director of fan-club services Jim Stabile says, "Everybody (wants) access to the best seats. That's the jewel in the crown of this whole thing."[3]

How can your organization create a structure that keeps you more connected with your customers, builds loyalty, and creates the "win-win," just as fan clubs do for recording artists?

Be Picky

In the early days of my professional speaking business, I worked at providing my "prospects" with a wide range of topics. I figured if I could provide programs on everything from time management to selling skills, from leadership to motivation, I would be able to get more bookings—and, therefore, more income.

The problem was, by taking *everything* that came along, I didn't create an identity for myself as a provider of quality information on *anything*. It wasn't until I started getting picky and focusing on just one thing—the creation of the experiences that ensure customer loyalty—that my speaking career blossomed. (Naturally, part of that was the fact that I have a laboratory in Obsidian Enterprises to put these principles into action.) If you aren't picky about what you do, customers won't be picking you.

If you aren't picky about what you do, customers won't be picking you.

As strange as it sounds, I believe that Wal-Mart is picky. It is not in the market for every person seeking a retail experience. It shoots for the segment of the buying public who seeks the best possible price/value ratio—and that is not everyone out there. Here's the proof: Target is picky too. It targets (pardon the pun) those who seek a balance between higher-quality merchandise and good value for their money. The applicable cliché here is "Jack-of-all-trades and master of none." The business that attempts to appeal to everyone will create loyalty from no one.

Keep It Simple

Too many times in business, we're our own worst enemy. We complicate things to the point of putting up roadblocks that deter prospects from doing business with us—thereby destroying any chance they will ever advance to "advocate" status.

Frankly, this isn't anything new to our culture. Confucius warned that simple language is best: "A gentleman is ashamed to let his words outrun his deeds. What need he to be a good talker? Those who down others with claptrap are seldom popular."

And we are seeing a movement toward more basic and simple approaches in many aspects of business. "A new trend in consumption may be contributing to declining retail sales" (according to University of Arkansas business researchers). Graduate student Helene Cherrier has been tracking this trend, called "voluntary simplicity," along with marketing faculty Jeff Murray and Norma Mendoza of the Sam M. Walton College of Business. "While value continues to be important, retailers should focus on the intangibles," said Mendoza, assistant professor of marketing, in a news release from the university. "If they emphasize service with the human touch and help consumers find the meaning behind the product or the purchase occasion, they can capitalize on their relationship to the community and to their loyal customers." In other words, get back to the simple act of developing relationships with customers.

Everyone loves simplicity . . . even highly sophisticated customers, like Wall Street investors. Consider the case of Cendant, the high-powered organization with holdings in travel, financial services, and real estate. *Business Week* reported in an October 11, 2002, article edited by Robin Ajello, that the company took a hit in share price—dropping from $20 in December 2001 to $11.25 in September 2002—chiefly because its financial statements were so difficult to read that investors couldn't process the information with a high degree of confidence.

Reexamine! Is it simple—pain free—for a customer to do business with you?

Reward the Right Results

My good friend Dr. Michael LeBoeuf wrote the classic business book when it comes to this point: *GMP—The Greatest Management Principle*.[4] As I stated in my first book, the "Greatest Management Principle" is: "Behavior rewarded is behavior repeated." As Dr. LeBoeuf clearly states, many times organizations are rewarding the wrong behavior without realizing it!

This point combines with the earlier point I made about measurement being one of the potential causes of a disconnection between you and your customer. How? Because, as discussed earlier, you get what you measure—*and* you reward based on those measurements!

Let's use the drive-thru restaurant as the example again. Let's say the home office assumes the customers make speed of service their main priority. Therefore, the executives at HQ develop the plan you might imagine—let's measure how long it takes for a customer to drive to the speaker, place the order, pay for the food, get the sack, and drive away. Makes sense, right?

So the manager of the Seymour, Indiana, restaurant gets the idea to really push to have the best time in speed of service to impress his bosses. He cracks the whip on his employees and tells them that nothing matters as much as getting cars through the process and out of the drive-thru lane as quickly as possible. With this in mind, his employees stop making small talk with customers so they'll move more quickly. They are in such a hurry now that they almost throw the bags of food into the customers' cars—because they've got to "keep 'em movin'!"

Because our manager has received the performance he wanted from his team, he rewards them for the speed at which they've "served" their customers. And at the next regional meeting, the Seymour manager is called on the stage to receive his incentive award check and a plaque to hang in his restaurant. All of the other managers are jealous, for they wanted to be the one receiving the recognition—and the award!

A strange thing happens back at the home office, though, once everyone returns from the meeting. Looking at sales figures, everyone is surprised to find that the Seymour store is losing business! How can that be? The executives decide that something must be done—and will be as soon as the manager returns from the vacation in Hawaii he's taking with his reward money! They'll tell him he's going to have to do more promotions, pass out more flyers, and figure out what in the world has gone wrong. No one ever realizes that the problem isn't with our manager—it's with the home office. They rewarded the wrong results.

Earlier in this chapter, I wrote an unflattering take on Verizon's statement regarding the customer experience. However, a recent development shows they are listening to their customer. When you examine the fine print in Verizon's newspaper ads, you'll note they indicate that offers promoted apply to both new *and* current customers. They'll provide the same incentive for steadfast customers as for new ones. By rewarding loyalty—guess what they will receive more of?

Start today to look at what your department, your team, your organization rewards. Remember, "Behavior rewarded is behavior repeated." If you measure the wrong activities—then reward the wrong results—you won't get what you want . . . you'll get what you rewarded.

Listen Hard and Talk Straight

There are more methods of communication now than ever in the history of mankind. Right now I'm sitting in a Starbucks in Henderson, Nevada, writing this chapter. Connected to the Internet as I sip my coffee via the T-Mobile Hotspot found in most of their locations, I've received twelve e-mails via Microsoft Entourage and four instant messages from Yahoo Messenger in the thirty minutes I've been here. Sitting on the table beside my laptop is my mobile phone, and I have already had two quick conversations. Your life may be much the same—we are overwhelmed with communication!

However, even though there are more *tools* than ever before, the *principles* of effective communication remain the same. Everyone wants to be listened to . . . and everyone wants his or her communication partner to be honest. What's so hard about that?

Plenty, evidently. When you consider the number of marriages ending in divorce in this country (to continue the personal relationship analogy), my guess is that few relationships are ending because the partners listened too intently and communicated with too much truthfulness. Now take into account how many of the relationships between customers and organizations are broken, and you will find the same pattern. Your customers aren't leaving you because you paid too much attention to what they were saying—or because you were too sincere and candid.

In an article called "Relationship Rehab: Open, Honest Communication Unlocks Success" featured in the July 2001 edition of *PR News*,

Diana Massaro, Vice President of Marketing at Solid Systems, a regional data hosting company in Houston, says that "open, honest and near-constant communication is the key to overcoming any glitches in the relationship."

She states in the article that she uses an Instant Messenger program to stay in constant contact with her PR agency so that she can address potential challenges almost before they occur in informal daily interactions. "We've been very honest about what's working—and what's not. We have conversations about everything to make sure things are right. It's open and honest communication about everything."

So, why—when there are so many tools available to us—do organizations and their people have so much difficulty in listening to customers? Obviously, there are a number of reasons: Time is compressed today and we're all too busy. There are multiple priorities to attend to. So much is going on and there is too much clutter, making it difficult to focus . . . and hundreds more.

These may be *reasons* for not listening, but they aren't *excuses*. There simply is no excuse for failing to listen to your customer!

In an article from *Communication World*, writer John R. Ward reports:

> Studies tell us that 70 to 80 percent of our waking life is spent communicating on some level. Of that time, 45 percent is listening, 30 percent speaking, 16 percent reading and 9 percent writing. If almost half our time is spent listening, and, since most people listen at the 25 percent level, imagine what you are missing. Listening is mostly an underdeveloped skill, one of the greatest gifts you can give to yourself for your future success and personal well-being. Good listening begins with the right attitude—cheerful, open, accepting. Unless somebody listens, there is no communication.[5]

If Ward is correct that listening is an underdeveloped skill, it stands to reason that by setting a priority to work on the skill and develop it to a greater level, we can take control of the situation. Before you send colleagues to seminars on enhanced listening . . . go to one for yourself. You, too, may be amazed at what you're missing.

Yet, listening isn't enough—it must be supported by straight talk with your customers and employees.

"You may think communication at your organization is already clear, complete and honest. But this may not be the case, according to research," reports *HR Focus* in its April 1, 2004, issue. The article titled "The Best Policy Now: Less 'Spin' and More Honesty," focused on a study done by consulting firm Towers Perrin.

The article continued: "Its recent survey, 'Enhancing Corporate Credibility: Is It Time to Take the Spin Out of Employee Communication?' notes: 'Of the 1,000 U.S. workers that participated, only 51% believe their employer generally tells employees the truth; 19% believe the opposite; and a third believe the information they receive today is less credible than it was just three years ago.'"

In their book, *The Day America Told the Truth*, authors James Patterson and Peter Kim found that most of the untruths told by people and organizations are not meant to hurt other people and, therefore, are relatively harmless.[6] However, it is the organization's—and therefore every manager's—responsibility to set the example and the standard in straight talk with customers. "If you've built your company on falsity, your own people won't tell you the truth," said Intuit founder Scott Cook in a *Fortune* magazine article written by Jerry Useem and published on December 20, 1999.

Preach What You Practice

While Reichheld is suggesting with this point of "preach what you practice" the importance of telling your story—a subject covered in great detail in my previous book—I think we need to expand the idea into being certain there is congruency between our "talk" and our "walk." There's an old poem by Edgar Guest that begins "I'd rather see a sermon than hear one any day." Preaching is done best by example. As the poem continues,

The eye's a better pupil and more willing than the ear;
Fine counsel is confusing, but example's always clear.

Often the disconnections that happen between customers and organizations occur because what the company is saying externally isn't what is being delivered.

Recently, my wife, Sheri, was battling some health problems and became very dehydrated. We called our doctor and were told that the best course of action was to go immediately to an emergency room and get Sheri treated with an IV of fluids. Being relatively new to the area—and our particular medical insurance not accepted at the closest hospital—we could have selected any emergency room in the city. We chose one that had wonderful ads on television speaking to the commitment this facility had to compassionate care for its patients. There were smiling doctors and patients in the television spot, and the hospital looked like a cross between a home in *Architectural Digest* and Disney World.

When we pulled into the hospital, a valet parking attendant greeted us—a wonderful service so that my ill wife didn't have to walk far and I didn't have to be away from her parking the car. We were off to a great start . . . it seemed there was a great deal of congruency between the preaching and the practice.

Imagine our disappointment to enter an emergency room area packed with people waiting for treatment! I didn't expect to encounter a perfect situation by any means, but neither did I anticipate a huge room filled with people hacking, coughing, moaning, and crying! The triage nurse who evaluated my wife's condition was surly—to put it nicely. She appeared to be much more concerned about my medical insurance than my wife's condition. Sheri, by now very weak and sick, cried and asked how long it was going to be before she would be assisted. Our doctor had told us she was going to telephone ahead and place the order for an IV, so we didn't really need to see a doctor; Sheri just needed to get "hooked up" by a nurse. The response: "We'll get to you when we can."

"How long will that be—do you have an estimate?" I asked.

"We'll get to you when we can."

I tried to politely explain that my wife was becoming sicker—her nausea almost uncontrollable—and all they had to do was to hook up the IV of saline that the doctor had ordered. It would provide enormous relief to her, and really wasn't a big deal, right?

"We'll get to you when we can."

After an hour of waiting, I approached the nurses' station. I asked if they might have a better idea of when Sheri was going to get assistance. Guess what the response was?

"We'll get to you when we can."

I don't want to reveal all of the horrors we saw that night—but, as an example, we saw a disheveled older man fall face-first out of his wheelchair onto the floor. When fellow patients and family rushed to help him and shouted for a nurse, we saw the woman at the station roll her eyes and say, "Hang on . . . give me a minute. I'm on the phone."

I called other emergency rooms and immediate care centers in the area and was told that since Sheri was so sick, the best thing was to wait there and hope—no sense getting out of line there to go someplace else and get in their line.

Finally after, unbelievably, *six hours* waiting in the emergency room, Sheri was called to see a doctor. The IV was hooked up, and she felt much, much better.

When I later called to complain about the treatment we received, there was absolutely zero empathy for our situation. More than a little hot under the collar, I asked if they ever watched their *own* television commercials—did they realize they were guilty, at a minimum, of false advertising?

"Oh, come on," the man on the other end of the conversation said dismissively. "No one believes those things." And, believe it or not, the feeling I received from this person was that it was *my* fault for trusting that there would be a linkage between their preaching and practicing.

Horrible, isn't it?

Before you decry the deterioration of health-care responsiveness, ask yourself this question: How congruent is *your* story with your execution?

Don't say, "Fly the friendly skies," then treat the flight attendants

Your customers do not think they are asking too much when they request that you *do* what you have promised.

who have to deliver on your catch-phrase like chattel. Don't say, "Complete satisfaction or the room is free," and then belittle the guest who brings you a problem. Don't say, "Your pizza in thirty minutes," then tell me when I place an order that "it's really busy tonight, so we'll see you in about an hour."

Your customers do not think they are asking too much when they request that you *do what you have promised.* If the focus is on low air-fares rather than personal, friendly service, then for goodness' sake, call it "fly the cheap skies."

By the way, the end of the story with the hospital is that they dis-covered I owed them more money—my co-pay was higher than they originally thought. When they called about payment, I told them to give the administrator with whom I had previously talked about my wife's treatment my answer: "We'll get to you when we can."

Man, that felt really good.

Many organizations *do* execute their promises—then keep it to themselves. Here's my question: If you aren't preaching about your practices, who is?

We all know several stories of corporate "folklore"—Fred Smith's first writing about his idea for FedEx in a college thesis; Southwest Airlines' genesis on a cocktail napkin, and many others—because those organizations tell their stories! If your company, department, or store fails to "preach" about what you do, how you do it, and what makes it unique, then it is *your* fault if customers fail to respond with loyalty!

But We *Have* to Prospect!

I certainly do not intend for this chapter to sound as though I—or your customers—believe you shouldn't prospect. Nothing could be farther from the truth. We all know you have to keep that "front door" open and continue to bring new customers in the door.

Yet many customers are a little scared about that. On one hand, customers hope that if you have more customers, you'll be able to provide a lower price. On the other, they fear that if you acquire even more customers, you'll give them less attention. If you have more customers, your business can grow, and that's good. Yet we customers also fear that if you grow too much, you'll forget about those of us who were here for you when you needed us.

So, from a practical standpoint, how does a business attract new customers—while continuing to eliminate the disconnection that exists when customers want to be loyal and not feel that you are endlessly prospecting?

Believe it or not, you'll find the roots of the answer in the same place I criticized in the beginning of this chapter: sales training.

"Unique Selling Proposition"

Another one of those points many of us were taught in sales training was the importance of the "unique selling proposition" (USP). In other words, what you had to do was to find the one point that would make your product or service different from your competitor's. What gave you the edge, and presented you with the opportunity to get the order and beat the competition?

Often this approach really came down to a couple of basic things: price and service. If my organization didn't have the lowest price, my "unique" proposition was that I was there for service after the sale. I was armed (through my training) with all kinds of lines that would enhance my "unique" offer. For example, "Well, everyone must set their own price because they know their product. So, if my competitor is cheaper than me—well, he knows the quality of his product better than I do!"

Or, if price was my ally, I could state, "Because we're bigger, we build more and therefore can produce more economically. We can make a better product for less money than their inferior product that will cost you more." Sound familiar?

An August 1, 1999, article by Rix Quinn in *Outdoor Power Equipment* cited the essentials for a USP: (1) unique in the field, (2) easily remembered, (3) simply stated and explained, and (4) important to the customer's life. All of these are obviously important to both the business and the customer.

However, the fundamental problem with the "unique selling proposition" is that, most of the time, what the organization considers "unique" does not meet that same standard with the customer. Clients have become so sophisticated, have so many more sources of information (like the Internet), and have heard so many "unique propositions" that what is being described as singularly exceptional is something they can probably find with relative ease someplace else.

Notice, as well, that nothing involved in the development of the USP says anything about the creation of loyalty. USP is a technique for making a sale. That's not a bad thing—but it just isn't enough in today's marketplace.

Another tool being discussed to a greater degree in management training (rather than sales training) is the "sustainable competitive advantage." Managers are asked what the superior position of their product or service is that can be both a differentiating factor between them and their competition—and maintained for an extended period of time.

The more I read about the "sustainable competitive advantage," the more I grow to realize the inherent problems with this approach, as well. When we ask the question, "what is there about my product that can truly be a competitive advantage we know can be sustained?" we continue to focus on the product or service and not the customer—unintentionally creating a disconnection we've previously discussed. Think about it—in today's remarkably fast-paced marketplace, there is practically *nothing* that can be sustained without continuous improvement. Therefore, it's virtually impossible to have a sustainable advantage without constantly refining the point that provides your differentiation.

Therefore, I would propose an approach that combines both a differentiated approach with the concern about life cycle and sustainability that will appeal to your customer's desires for loyalty: the "Continuous Compelling Advantage" (CCA).

The Continuous Compelling Advantage

First, *what is a competitive advantage?* Competitive advantage is the position that is achieved "when a firm's product is viewed by its customers as having a higher value than the product of its competitors," according to business author and educator M. E. Porter.[7]

In addition, continuous improvement can make successful replication by your competitors extremely unlikely, because you have created a moving target. Barbara Flynn in the September 21, 1996, issue of *Journal of Managerial Issues* wrote, "The imitating firm is attempting to duplicate a performance level the target firm will soon surpass. Continuous improvement is based upon the consistent and additive advantages of many changes that complicate a firm's processes and systems, thereby making it difficult for other firms to imitate them." In other words, the execution of a strategy of continuous improvement powerfully creates a competitive advantage for an organization.

And, as we've previously discussed, customers seek an emotional connection with the organizations where they do business if they're to become loyal advocates. The compelling aspect of the CCA means you are developing an approach that goes beyond a "selling proposition" and creates a "loyalty strategy."

The CCA is an approach that combines the need for differentiation on the part of the organization with the need for emotional connection on the part of the customer. It addresses the organization's desire to have an advantage over the competition, and the customer's desire to be loyal to a consistent, dependable provider. The focus of the CCA is how an organization can deliver what the customer really wants— and not merely what makes a product or service different.

Most important, the CCA serves the dual purpose of being a tool that enhances customer loyalty while attracting new customers at the same time.

One of the main strengths of the CCA is that it is built through simplicity—yet its implications are deep and profound within an organization. To build your CCA, you begin by working your way through three questions:

1. What *advantages* do our products or services have over our competitors' in the marketplace?

2. Which of these advantages create *compelling* reasons for customers to do business with us instead of our competitors—and how do we communicate them?

3. How do we create a *continuous*, never-ending cycle of enhancing our advantages, making them even more compelling, and communicating our differentiation to customers?

Let's examine the three questions in greater detail:

First, *what are your advantages?* If you don't know, why should your customer? (By the way, my experience over the past two decades working with organizations has been that it is not that a company can't identify advantages—it is that the advantages it thinks are important often don't have significant traction with its customers.)

For example, if you are a hotel chain, you may view your advantages as those amenities in the room that differentiate you from your competition. Westin Hotels launched a major effort to communicate that its showers are better. At Westin, $10 million was spent to add dual showerheads with five settings that can potentially deliver twice as much water as a single showerhead. The hotel chain also added a curved rod that makes the shower curtain bulge out—and gives bathers more space—and a fifty-nine-by-thirty-two-inch Brazilian cotton bath towel to their rooms.

According to *USA Today*, Starwood Hotels—parent company of Westin—is counting on what it dubs "The Heavenly Shower" to lure guests from other hotel chains. The newspaper reported, "Jon Kimball, general manager of the Westin Los Angeles Airport, thinks it will be a hit on Los Angeles' Century Boulevard, which is lined with hotels from competing brands.

"'This is the most competitive strip I've ever worked,' he says, 'and if you have a point of differentiation, then it puts you at an advantage to attract the seasoned traveler.'"[8]

Achieving an advantage through differentiation from your competitors is certainly nothing new in American business. In 1933, Harvard University Press published an essay by Edward H. Chamberlain titled "The Theory of Monopolistic Competition." In this paper, Chamberlain's fundamental point is that an organization should want to be distinct enough in the marketplace to attract a higher percentage of customers than its competitors—yet not so unique in location, product, or price to alienate potential customers.

In other words, to borrow the term of Westin's Kimball, what are the *points* of differentiation? What are those benefits that give you some distinction in the marketplace? Remember, it doesn't have to be wildly revolutionary—it simply (at this point) needs to be a distinguishing aspect. Write down those fine points that create space between you and your competition.

Second, *which of these advantages create a compelling reason for the customer to become loyal?*

This will be a difficult question for most managers—because many of us tend to focus on the feature, not the benefit (to use sales training terms). Many may say that the fifty-nine-by-thirty-two-inch Brazilian cotton bath towel is a compelling reason for loyalty. It's not. It is the *better shower experience* that is persuasive.

If you are having a difficult time getting a handle on what makes something *compelling*, a great standard is developed in marketing professor Leonard L. Berry's book, *On Great Service: A Framework for Action* (Free Press, 1995). He states that a significant test for a business to measure the "compelling" concept is to ask, "If we suddenly, magically disappeared, would our customers miss us?"

He's exactly right. If a differentiation point you've mentioned did not exist—or no longer existed—would your customer notice? If you went away entirely, would your customers merely shrug and find another supplier—or would they feel emotionally disappointed? If you don't have points that differentiate you from your competition—and create a significant connection with your customers—then you won't be missed. (Think here of companies like Eastern Airlines, products like "Crystal Pepsi" and "New Coke," . . . or the "comeback" attempt of rapper Vanilla Ice.) In these cases, moving to the competitor simply provides the same—or better—results for the customer.

However, when you have the kind of differentiation that creates an emotional impact, you create loyalty *and* attract new business.

Third, *how do we create a continuous, never-ending cycle of enhancing our advantages?* The goal of this final question is to focus you and your organization on the experiences that create loyalty instead of the features that provide an insignificant, short-term advantage. For example, if Westin decides that creating the better shower experience can become a CCA, it will focus its efforts on maintaining leadership with a myriad of new products, bathroom design, and engineering efforts to be known as the ultimate leader in this area. If it focuses just on the towels, it no longer has a CCA. If towels are thought to be Westin's competitive advantage, then all Marriott has to do is buy bigger Brazilian cotton towels, and Westin is now in second place. That's not a "continuous" advantage.

However, if Westin says it now has an advantage—a differentiating factor—in terms of where they are now with the "shower experience," and commits its efforts and resources to having a "continuous compelling advantage" in that area, it will naturally approach the issue with a customer-oriented focus.

Let's use the airlines as another example. When Southwest began its rise to the top of the airline battle, it combined low fares and a fun approach to flights to create a CCA. Other competitors could (and did) match the fares, but they couldn't match the "continuous compelling advantage" that Southwest had—the differentiation it enjoyed by the combination of low fares and fun. In fact, Southwest even named its prices "Fun Fares." Other airlines attempted telling jokes, acting just as Southwest does, but it had the same impact as hearing one comedian doing another's routine. It wouldn't seem right if a new comic came along and did Tim Allen's brilliant material about power tools. Same thing is true with another airline attempting to perform just like Southwest.

jetBlue entered the marketplace and—to its everlasting credit—did not attempt to simply duplicate Southwest. It knew and executed the principles discussed in this chapter—it created a CCA. jetBlue combined low fares with assigned seats (something Southwest doesn't provide)—and, as a major differentiation, put television screens at each seat with DirecTV satellite service.

Note that both Southwest and jetBlue have low fares. Why fly one over the other? It depends on what passenger experience you find more compelling. Other airlines seem to fail to understand this vital point.

For example, United Airlines started its low fare spin-off, "Ted," to compete with Southwest and jetBlue. The problem is, Ted used the same flight attendants as the mainline United—and then required these flight attendants instruct passengers to watch "TedVision" and listen to "Ted Tunes." The result is an experience that is, in my opinion, awfully bland. It alienates the loyal customers of United who have chosen that airline because they don't want to fly another Southwest imitator—and doesn't create a CCA that will attract business away from the low-fare competitors Ted is attempting to challenge. Through the "endless prospecting" efforts of Ted, United has driven away many loyal customers.

I should add that one of the loyal customers put off by Ted is yours truly. I was so upset by the ridiculous decision to create Ted that I started a Web site, www.DontFlyTed.com. As a loyal customer who flew United Airlines more than one hundred thousand miles every year for about a decade, I could not believe that any organization—especially one in bankruptcy—would spend so much money to create a pale imitation of successful airlines that it wasn't going to overcome anyway, and cast off so many devoted patrons in the process. As aviation consultant Mike Boyd joked about Ted, "It's not a strategy, it's a paint job."[9]

CCA

We will return to the concept of the CCA several more times in this book, but for now focus on the three questions that build the foundation of a Continuous Compelling Advantage.

It's important to note that the CCA not only means your customers are around a lot longer—the chances are it means your organization will be too! In an *Insurance Journal* (April 19, 2004) article titled, "Now What! A Look Back At Lessons Learned from the 1990's" by Kevin Kelley, chairman and CEO of Lexington Insurance and a senior vice president at American International Group, this aspect of "survive and thrive" was noted:

> Staying power [for a company] can only be achieved by having a number of compelling and sustainable competitive advantages coupled with the balance that a well-diversified, smart, integrated set of . . . products can bring, along with the management to maximize their opportunity. In a world that is constantly changing, dealing with a [customer] on a continuous basis is valuable. The extra value that comes from a continuous relationship is multifaceted. Communication is easier. Expectations are realistic. Knowing whom to call is a value that is hard to quantify but nevertheless increases during times of uncertainty and change.

Remember the basic premise: customers want to be loyal, and the businesses that understand that point and exploit it (in a truly positive sense) through the development of Continuous Compelling Advantages are visionary and remarkable. Take eBay as an example: Meg Whitman says, "Loyalty is the special ingredient in eBay's sauce." And, as the aforementioned author of *Loyalty Rules*, Frederick Reichheld, states, "An increase in customer retention rates of 5% increases profit 25% to 95%."[10]

Does that sound interesting to you?

Executive Summary

The Third Disconnection is that what customers REALLY want is reciprocal loyalty—yet most organizations appear to be endlessly prospecting for new customers, often at the expense of their current ones.

- Customer retention is the most important goal your organization can develop.

- In a blind attempt to acquire additional customers, many organizations make offers to attract new business that they do not extend to their current, loyal customers.
- Perhaps it isn't surprising that most businesses will lose ONE-HALF of their customers within a five-year period.
- Customers have rights! They have the right to expect an organization to live up to their promises, to meet the expectations they set for their customers and to treat clients with empathy and respect.

- Our traditions about sales often block the development of compelling customer experiences.
  - In sales training, we're often taught that "sales is a numbers game" and that we should just keep on "cold-calling" until we can get the prospect to the point of closing.
  - Even the term "closing" implies success in selling—and the end of a relationship.
    - When a relationship is over, we seek closure. Yet, closing is thought of as a positive thing in the vernacular of selling. Often closing is thought of as overcoming the prospect's objections and the use of manipulative techniques to move the prospect to action. However, unless we create value, we can win the sale and lose the relationship.
- Relationships mean reciprocal loyalty.
  - In a personal relationship, we would not be loyal to someone who isn't focused upon us. Why would it be any different in a professional one?
  - The Six Pillars of Character describe the essential elements we need to understand to build lasting relationships: *trustworthiness, respect, responsibility, fairness, caring, citizenship.*
  - By clearly exhibiting these traits, we display our character and create relationships through the integrity of our actions.

- Building customer loyalty
  - It doesn't matter how many new customers you are attracting to come in the front door if you are losing more out of the back one! Retention of customers is the vital element of ongoing organizational success.
  - How does your customer acquisition strategy "set the table" for long-term relationships with your customers?
    - What happens to them once your prospects become customers? Are they handled with as much care and concern as they were during the acquisition phase?
  - The more interactive the interaction is with you and your customers, the greater the likelihood that you will build customer loyalty. Your organization must accurately assess the depth of commitment of your customers.
  - There are Six Stages of Customer Interaction:
    1. *Suspect*: A potential buyer who needs more information about you—and you about her—to see if there is a possible fit upon which a relationship could be built.
    2. *Prospect*: Someone who has yet to purchase your product or service, yet with whom you have something in common. This could be a product/service fit—or, it could be something on a personal level.
    3. *First-time buyer*: One who has used your services once— and is considering whether or not to do it again.
    4. *Repeat customer*: One who isn't dynamically or emotionally engaged with your organization, but has chosen to make additional purchases from you.
    5. *Client*: A repeat customer with whom you have an emotional connection. Someone who asks not only for your product, but for your advice and counsel and views your organization as a resource and partner in their growth.
    6. *Advocate*: A client who is such a "raving fan" that they recommend you to their friends and colleagues.

The key for any company is to cultivate customers and prospects through the six stages to create opportunity and rewards for moving up the ladder into becoming an advocate for your organization.

- Organizations can find enormous value in enhancing customer loyalty.
  - Research indicates that the retention of a mere 5 percent of those customers you were going to lose creates "an increase in the value of an average customer by 25 to 100%" according to author Frederick Reichheld.
  - Reichheld's six-point plan for enhancing customer loyalty is:
    1. *Play to win-win:* Customer loyalty will not be created if you are trying to win at their expense.
    2. *Be picky:* Organizations that try to be everything to everybody inspire loyalty from no one.
    3. *Keep it simple:* Simplicity implies ease of transaction and relational comfort. Complexity does not create loyalty.
    4. *Reward the right results:* As Dr. Michael LeBoeuf says, "Behavior rewarded is behavior repeated."
    5. *Listen hard and talk straight:* Focus on the needs and wants of your customers—communicate with them forthcomingly.
    6. *Preach what you practice:* Tell the story of your organization's efforts so you gain other loyal customers.

- Create a "Continuous Compelling Advantage" (CCA).
  - There must be more than a competitive advantage that you hold over your competition—loyalty is inspired by a compelling reason to do business with you.
  - Imitation of successful competitors fails to provide that compelling reason for a customer to choose you.

○ By creating a CCA, you expand the life span of your product or service, differentiate yourself from your competition, build relationships, and enhance customer loyalty.

Bridge Building
Moving from Endless Prospecting to Reciprocal Loyalty

- Do you truly believe that customers want to be loyal, or do you believe that they are always "shopping" you against your competitor?

- Could your response to the previous question reveal a self-fulfilling prophecy regarding the customer interaction you have?

- Do you have a better deal for new customers than you offer to existing customers?

- Do you ever excuse your delivery of products or services because of "how tough it is to do what you do"?
    - ○ Do you find that acceptable when *you* are a customer?

- Think for a moment and describe your philosophy of sales. Are customers and their objections something to be overcome? How do you view the process of closing?

- Outline how your organization and your people exemplify the Six Pillars of Character:
    - ○ Trustworthiness
    - ○ Respect
    - ○ Responsibility
    - ○ Fairness
    - ○ Caring
    - ○ Citizenship

- What is your organization's strategy to move customers from Suspects to Advocates?

- In your own words—and ask others in your organization to do the same—describe the value of customer loyalty to your company.

- Do you prospect transparently? In other words, is prospecting for new customers done in such a way that your current clients don't feel slighted? (Imagine being at a reception where the person you are talking with always has his eyes on the move, looking for someone else to speak with instead of you. That's the feeling customers get from endless prospecting.)

- Why are soft skills now just as important as the hard skills that have been so valued in the traditional organization for so many years?

- The CCA (Continuous Compelling Advantage) is vitally important for your organization's ability to enhance customer loyalty, and obtain new customers as well. Describe it.

- What is the CCA that your organization offers to your clients and prospects?

4

THE FOURTH DISCONNECTION

What Customers REALLY Want: *Differentiation*
What Business Offers: *Sameness*

You're in your rental car, driving down a main thoroughfare in a strange city. As you look for your hotel, you suddenly have that sense of déjà vu. You really believe you've been here before—even though you know you haven't.

Then you realize why you're having this experience: everything looks similar. There are McDonald's and Wendy's, Barnes & Noble and Borders, even Bank of America and US Bank. In some ways, that's good—it's just like home. However, in many ways it's not so hot. There's no differentiation between this town and any other—it's just like home.

In a previous chapter, we discussed the importance of sensation as an element in creating powerful customer experiences. If you travel any significant amount at all, I am willing to bet this sensation sounded familiar.

In his terrific book *Fast Food Nation*,[1] Eric Schlosser uses the major fast food companies to describe the homogenization of America. In one way, all the fast-food companies did was follow the migration of population centers as the interstate highway system made our country more mobile and automobile-dependent. In another way, however, they were a great part of changing the culture. Previously, communities had significant variation from one another, because the businesses in those cities and towns were diverse. However, when every place to eat in your town is the same as in mine, our towns become very comparable.

Yet there is a safety in sameness. Many organizations find a great deal of comfort in the fact that the product or service they offer is a "commodity." In other words, they are in a business that—as Joshua Kennon writes in *Investing for Beginners*—"much like wheat or corn competes primarily on the basis of price (you don't go to the supermarket to buy bread made from Farmer Joe's wheat)."[2] When you view yourself as a commodity business, you are also—in essence—attempting to give yourself and your organization a pass on the challenge of differentiation.

However, we clearly see that some businesses find a way to transcend commoditization. They discover a path out of the maze of just offering a bland, unremarkable product or service. For example, money is no doubt a commodity. A dollar is a dollar is a dollar . . . right?

Well, no. It's pretty important to a plethora of businesses how you obtain, invest, spend, and manage that dollar. Let's look at one use, a mortgage for your home. If you have a mortgage of, for example, $500,000, that half million dollars is the same money no matter whom you choose as a lender. Money is a commodity at its most basic level—however we can easily find mortgage brokers and bankers who find a way to differentiate that $500k and everything surrounding it so that you will select them as your lender of choice.

Mortgage Banker magazine reports in their October 1990 edition that, according to research with focus groups by Ann Arbor–based Washtenaw Mortgage Company, 70 to 80 percent of every borrower's decision making begins by discussing price. Therefore, without service and innovative customer experiences that create differentiation, the entire mortgage process merely becomes a customer holding an auction.

The only—and I mean *only*—approach that will transcend this commoditization is understanding that borrowing to finance a home is not just about money. Customers have proved that they want more from their mortgages; according to the *Mortgage Banker* article by Richard Greene, vice president of marketing at The Washtenaw Mortgage

Company, customers have clearly demonstrated that (when presented the option) they also want to purchase financial advice, good communications, fast service, security, comfort, and professionalism.

Greene states:

> Mortgage companies that define their corporate mission in terms of making a greater volume of mortgage at better spreads end up auctioning off their product to the lowest bidder. As lenders contemplate their company's policies regarding the internal sale, they approach the central question for mortgage companies. Are we selling mortgages, generic financial products, or are we selling mortgage *services*—a financial product bundled with communications, counseling and problem-solving services?

Mortgage brokers and bankers can find a way to transcend commodity by taking the focus away from product and price and putting it on uniqueness and differentiation—what customers REALLY want. As I suggested earlier, those organizations that choose not to differentiate and remain the same old commodity are simply saying they have neither the desire nor the intellectual curiosity to make their offerings remarkable. Companies in just about every industry have displayed extraordinary success by implementing a creative approach to an old product.

The most blatant example is Starbucks. Getting a cup of java is hardly a novel idea, yet Starbucks differentiated a commodity—coffee.

Evian differentiated the ultimate commodity of all—*water*! Even now, the marketing muscles of Pepsi (through Aquafina) and Coke (through Dasani) work to create a unique brand of the ultimate commodity. Just a few days ago, I caught myself standing in a convenience store, slowly scanning the cooler, looking for my favorite brand of water! Heaven forbid I should get a drink out of the water fountain over in the corner—I wanted my favorite!

If businesses can find a strategy for differentiating a cup of coffee— or, for goodness' sake, *water*—you can find a way to differentiate *your* product or service, no matter the size or scope of your business.

"What does it matter?" you might ask. "We compete solely on price. How in the world do you differentiate [insert your product here]?"

First, I have to ask this: Why would any business *choose* to compete as a commodity? These companies are usually exemplified by huge capital expenditures (in relation to production), low profit margins, and intense competition. Why play that game if you don't have to?

Yet many companies are so grounded in the commodity trap that they keep doing what they're doing because they've always been doing it. (Organizations, as well as people, can be creatures of habit.) However, some businesses break out of that prison—and discover remarkable success by providing what customers REALLY want.

More on Obsidian Enterprises

We have heard forever about persons suffering from low self-esteem, but we've never really examined the fact that there are companies with this challenge as well. It seems as though every time we purchase a company through Obsidian, there is a meeting where someone from our new acquisition will say something that drives me absolutely nuts!

First, a little more about Obsidian: We are a publicly traded (NASDAQ:OTC: OBDE) holding company that invests in and acquires small and mid-cap companies in basic industries such as manufacturing and transportation. Headquartered in Indianapolis, Indiana, we at Obsidian Enterprises currently conduct business through six subsidiaries: Classic Manufacturing, Inc., a manufacturer of commercial, racing, and recreational trailers; Danzer Industries, Inc., a manufacturer of cargo trailers and service and utility truck bodies and accessories; Obsidian Conference & Catering Center, a meeting and special event facility and caterer; Pyramid Celebrity Coaches, Inc., a leading provider of corporate and celebrity entertainer coach leases; United Trailers, a manufacturer of steel-framed cargo, racing, ATV, and specialty trailers; and U.S. Rubber Reclaiming, Inc., a butyl rubber reclaiming operation.

Obsidian looks to acquire historically profitable, small- and middle-market companies that operate in niche markets of basic industries. We use the same investment strategy we have previously employed successfully as private equity investors. The key elements of this strategy are customer focus, differentiation, investment discipline, smaller target investments, transaction control, broad management experience, diversification, strong origination capabilities, and active management.

We also have several affiliated companies, all or part of which we have acquired through private investments. These affiliated companies are varied and include The Aesthetic Surgery Center, a cosmetic surgery practice; Champion Trailer, a manufacturer of fully customized, all-aluminum race car transporters and hospitality and corporate display trailers; Fair Finance, a business financial services and consumer investing company; Speedster Motorcars, manufacturer of 1936 Auburn Boat-tail Speedster replicas and other classic car replicas; Square One Graphics, a motor graphics specialist company located in Indianapolis; and Vizion Restaurant & Vapour Lounge, an upscale place to dine, drink, and dance in Indianapolis.

After Obsidian acquires a business, it almost always seems that someone on the other side of the table with the organization with which we are now involved will state, "Well, you have to understand, we're in a commodity business." That's the point where I just want to jump across the table and strangle someone! This thinking drives me *nuts*!

You Don't *Have* to Be a Commodity!

I honestly believe there is *no* business that *has* to be solely a commodity business. I believe many organizations have chosen—either through preference, tradition, or inaction—to play the commodity game.

Look, I understand that the trend in every industry is, at some point, to drift toward commoditization. Believe it or not, it has even happened in the purely service industry in which I'm very involved—professional speaking.

When speaker Cavett Robert decided in 1972 that there should be a way for professional speakers to communicate with one another and develop standards in their industry, he called several friends to have a meeting that became the genesis of the National Speakers Association (NSA).

Cavett Robert was a larger-than-life figure, both on the stage and in personal contact. By 1976, Cavett—through the sheer force of his personality—had rounded up 189 speakers to attend the first national convention of the association. The industry of professional speakers at corporate and association meetings was then in its infancy. Cavett Robert stood before the group and told them he had a vision for an organization where professional speakers could convene to improve their presentations, exchange ideas, and share experiences. He felt that everyone involved in the speaking profession would benefit from growing the number and quality of professional speakers. He referred to it as "making a bigger pie." And that "bigger pie" philosophy guided the industry—and its trade association—for the next quarter century.

As the NSA grew in membership and outreach—and as the industry it represented grew and matured (in great part because of the association's efforts)—a very interesting trend started. All of a sudden, the pie wasn't growing as rapidly—and one heck of a lot more people were showing up to eat pie.

When I sent out my first promotional mailing—a brochure sent to one hundred prospective customers advertising my services as a professional speaker back in 1981—I received ninety-two responses! Almost every caller said, "Wow! We've never received a mailing from a professional speaker before." Now, meeting planners will receive one or two every *day* from the literally thousands of professional speakers in the country. And, as you might imagine, the niche industry of professional speaking started to experience what every other industry does at a point of maturation and commoditization: suppliers (the speakers) and buyers (meeting planners) became focused on price and processing speed.

Pricing pressures became—for the first time—a significant experience in the profession. Meeting planners often indicated that they were selecting the speaker for their meeting based on a difference of fifty to a hundred dollars!

And in an industry where the standard lead time on a booking (the number of days between the booking of the engagement and the actual presentation) was at least six months, we now discovered that, for convenience' sake, customers were booking less than *six weeks* out!

When I asked one meeting planner who had selected me to speak to her convention of more than a thousand people why she waited until ten days before the meeting to secure a speaker, her response was chilling: "Well, *somebody* good was going to be open." She saw little difference between one speaker and another. Speakers were now a commodity.

My guess is that Cavett Robert never imagined so many people would want to "eat the pie" of professional speaking and the industry would change so dramatically. But it has.

The only speakers who have seen a dramatic increase in business and fees are celebrity speakers and best-selling authors. The reason is obvious: they're differentiated, branded, not a commodity . . . even though their product (a speech) is basically the same product as those professionals who are seeing tremendous erosion in the profitability of their businesses. It's a metaphor for every industry: if you're not different, you're a commodity.

But stop and think why that maxim is true. The only reason those in the speaking, airline, sporting goods—whatever!—industries that are differentiated and branded as more profitable and have a more sustainable situation must be because customers tend to *prefer* their differentiation to the sameness of a commodity! If customers didn't want it—if they didn't prefer it—they wouldn't be willing to pay more for it! They wouldn't be willing to seek it out even though it was often less convenient than the commodity version of the product or service.

We've already discussed some areas in which differentiation works for companies. This chapter will provide a tighter focus on its impact and recommend strategies on developing differentiation as a critical factor for all businesses—especially those presumed to be of a commodity type.

> It's a metaphor for every industry: if you're not different, you're a commodity.

Keys to a Commodity Business

Let's examine a basic of business: What is a commodity? Perhaps by reexamining what a commodity is, we can avoid the pitfall of becoming (or remaining) one. Experts suggest that there are three aspects to understanding commodity:

1. Price

2. Quality

3. Service

Price

Are you the absolute cheapest in your industry? Are you the lowest-priced provider your customers can discover? Well, I now have a strategy for how I can beat you in the marketplace. All I have to do to topple you is cut my price.

Don't get me wrong—I'm not suggesting for a moment that customers have no regard for your pricing policy. I do not believe that they buy without a consideration of the price of your product or service. However, I do believe that infinitely too often, organizations offer price, when what the customer REALLY wants is something more.

If you pick up the most recent edition of *Fortune* magazine that lists the five hundred biggest companies in America, you will find the number one organization is not software giant Microsoft or a big manufacturer like General Motors. It's Wal-Mart. Amazing, isn't it? A discount retailer with a home office in a small town in Arkansas is the biggest company in America.

Because Wal-Mart is number one—and its corporate tag line (or "High Concept") is "low prices everyday"—it's easy to assume that the pathway to success for Wal-Mart has been to become the price leader in every category, right?

Well, that's only a *part* of the story . . . and much less of the story than you might imagine. Perhaps the best way to analyze this is not to look at Wal-Mart, but instead to look at its competitors. The two that first come to mind are Kmart and Target.

Target has become highly successful by refusing to play the commodity-mentality price game with Wal-Mart. By choosing a different path, it has emerged as a strong competitor. It does not view the products it sells as commodities. Sure, the box of Tide is the same everywhere, yet Target's approach is that the store in which you buy your detergent is not.

The most illustrative example, however, is Kmart. And here's the fundamental question: If price is the point of ultimate importance, why is Wal-Mart number one on the "Fortune 500" and Kmart went into bankruptcy? Are the prices between the two so dissimilar, so out of line from each other, that the shopper has no choice but to go to Wal-Mart?

Obviously not. Both stores are within a few pennies of each other on just about every item. Customers voted with their feet and their pocketbooks and chose Wal-Mart precisely because it *wasn't* Kmart! (Remember, Kmart was, in most communities, there first.) Customers wanted to shop at a store that was better lit and maintained. They enjoyed being welcomed by the "greeter" at the front of every store. Because the prices were so similar, shoppers decided to spend their hard-earned dollars where they could take pleasure in the superior customer experience.

I've often noted that I believe the greatest "head fake" in the history of American business was Sam Walton preaching his gospel of "low prices everyday." If you want to throw off your defender in sports, you give them a head fake. A receiver will head-fake a cornerback, go a different direction, and make the reception. A head fake in basketball gets the person guarding you to jump a bit too soon, giving you the chance to drive around him or get off an open shot.

In business, Walton's "head fake" was to continually announce that the most important point of his business was the supposedly lower price of just about every item in the store than the competition's—then he put a greeter up front to welcome every customer into his own place of business. He developed a passion among employees about the company—and a loyal following to him, personally, as well. Wal-Mart became an employer of choice in many communities . . . important not just for human resources issues, but also because these employees would then tell their neighbors what a great place Wal-Mart was to work and shop.

Meanwhile, the national chain competitors—like Kmart and Montgomery Ward, as well as countless local retailers that were feeling the impact of Wal-Mart's growth—bit on Walton's head fake. As their market shares dwindled, they figured it must be the pricing that was attracting their former customers to Wal-Mart.

So the competitors cut their prices, reduced their margins . . . and many went broke. Ward's is out of business completely, and Kmart had to work through bankruptcy. They bit on Sam Walton's head fake. They failed to understand the major importance of a minor player like a greeter . . . of store design and lighting that create an experience . . . of getting hometown folks to love their jobs while the store they worked in was putting their neighbor out of business. No doubt, price was a factor, but it wasn't the *total* reason by a long shot.

The recent passing of former president Ronald Reagan reminds us of a similar analogy. Reagan increased defense spending—and the Soviet Union, believing that it must continue to play the same game, attempted to keep pace . . . right up to the point that the USSR collapsed.

Wal-Mart's competitors Kmart and Montgomery Ward did the same as the Soviets. It's like Monopoly, where you keep playing until every competitor but one is broke. (With the recent transaction that combines Kmart with legendary retailer Sears, it will be fascinating to observe if this new alliance will stimulate creative-thinking approaches.) The adage is that you either win or lose.

It is interesting to see big-box home-improvement retailer Home Depot delicately moving away from a focus on price. Remember when its advertising slogans were "Where low prices are just the beginning" and "Driving down the cost of home improvement"? Now Home Depot rallies around the phrase "You can do it; we can help." Hmmm—nothing about price? Well, there's a reason.

Home Depot's leadership—such as its brilliant CEO Bob Nardelli—knows that there is another alternative: decide not to play the commodity game. No company should target being the cheapest in the marketplace as a long-term strategy for success—because price is never a long-term play.

Don't believe that? Here's a bit of history—and a chance to show my age: Are you old enough to remember when Sony products were cheap? The tag "Made in Japan" meant, at the time, that the product would be lower priced and inexpensively produced. Yet Sony understood that being the cheapest isn't a long-term strategy, and now it is the most expensive in many of its product lines . . . and *highly* successful.

As Ellen Rohr wrote in *Entrepreneur* magazine:

> Don't even think about using low prices to attract customers. Actually, the market is much less price-sensitive than you think it is. The market bears all kinds of prices. Can you believe people pay $50,000 for a watch? Three dollars for a bottle of water? Hundreds of dollars for pro wrestling tickets? Consumers will buy just about anything if they can see the value or benefit. The market doesn't set prices . . . *marketers* do! What makes you special?[3]

Many commodity businesses have to be price leaders because they are neither creative enough to add value to their product or service, nor customer-focused enough to create the kinds of experiences customers REALLY want. That's a strong statement—but one I truly believe.

It's funny—when I make that statement at a presentation, the only people who argue about it are the ones who have only attempted the commodity/price approach. The ones who have moved from price leader to focusing on what their customers REALLY want have never contested my assertion.

If price is truly your core focus, you have chosen to play the commodity game—and you are in a trap.

Quality

It's long been assumed that to break free of the price-focused mentality and approach, an organization must improve the quality of its products and services beyond that offered by the commodity players.

Quality is important—yet subjective. And even the term *subjective* doesn't truly describe what customers are doing. If I believe customers make a subjective judgment about the quality of the product I'm offering, I've once again allowed my business to fall into the product-focus trap we discussed in an earlier chapter.

For example, let's say you operate three dry-cleaning stores in a mid-size town. A bigger competitor has the approach that the dry cleaning of dress shirts for office employees is nothing more than a commodity. So the competitor lowers the cost of cleaning a dress shirt to $1.29.

Of course, you—as a business professional who understands that price is not the sole answer—respond by improving the excellence of your cleaning. Sure, you charge $1.99, but you do the extras that make your dry cleaning of a higher standard. You place tissue paper over the hanger so the shirt doesn't get hanger lines. You place little plastic cuff links in shirts with French cuffs so they retain a sharp fold.

This added quality provides the differentiation we discussed earlier, right? Well, the answer is a definite "maybe."

How friendly are your employees? How do you market your enhanced quality? How do you provide not just higher-quality dry cleaning, but a significantly enhanced dry-cleaning *experience* to your customer that is compelling and significantly better than your commodity-minded competition? If customers have to wait in line a long time and be met by undereducated, slow employees at the counter, the value of the higher quality in cleaning is greatly diminished.

One of my best friends, Mark Mayfield, is a humorist and author from Kansas City. Driving to the airport to catch a flight for a speech, Mark stopped at the dry cleaners to pick up a shirt he had dropped off the previous day. In fact, since Mark was only going to be gone overnight for the speech, he had not packed a shirt in his suitcase—he was going to take the shirt from the cleaners and drop it in his bag on the way to the airport and wear that one for his presentation.

As Mark waited in the store, the owner/manager of the small cleaners brought out Mark's shirt. Mark then walked to his car, popped open the trunk, and removed the plastic dry cleaning bag to place his shirt in his luggage. To his surprise and chagrin, there were two huge rips in the shirt—making it totally unwearable!

Mark stormed back into the cleaners and—filled with both adrenaline and testosterone—pointed his finger at the shirt and then at the owner. "Look at this! I'm rushing to the airport, and now I don't have a shirt for my trip! This is awful! What are *you* going to do about it?"

The owner examined the shirt and shook his head. "I am *so* sorry," he replied. "I know who did this—and I will take care of it."

"*How?*" Mark demanded. "*How* are you going to take care of this?"

"Well," came the reply, "I know exactly the person who made the error . . . and I'm going to take her out back and shoot her." Mark reports that the owner never smiled, but paused a beat and continued. "It's my mom," he said. "I mean . . . I'll miss her, but I can't put up with this lack of quality."

All of a sudden, Mark started laughing. And the dry cleaner did too. As they stood there, Mark suddenly realized it was only a shirt. The dry cleaner had created an experience—and continued to do so. "Here," he said, "write down for me where you're staying tonight. I'll take care of everything." When Mark arrived at the hotel in Chicago and entered his room, not only was there a small plate of fruit and cheese, but there was also a new white dress shirt in Mark's size and a note from the dry cleaner, saying, "Thanks for your business—it means a lot to me."

Guess where Mark Mayfield gets every stitch of clothing cleaned to this day? Do you think he believes that all dry cleaners are exactly the same?

Now, I'm not insinuating that *all* we need to do is to enhance the quality of the products and services we provide. Yet—as my buddy Mark can testify—you can grow your business to a significant degree if you also focus on improving the quality of the relationships you establish with your customers as you improve the quality of your product and service.

If you restrict your definition of quality to that of your product, you miss out on what customers really want—and you reinforce the movement toward commodity. If I'm your competitor and improved quality of product or service is all that matters, then all I have to do is start putting tissue paper on the hangers.

From a product standpoint, does jetBlue provide higher-quality transportation than Southwest? I guess it depends on whether you'd rather be on an Airbus or a Boeing 737. Would you prefer to have a flight service team dressed in khaki shorts, telling jokes and having a great time—or to watch your own television? It's up to you. However, I would suggest that *both* these competitors understand that customers *blend* the quality of your product with the quality of your service—and focus on the quality of the *total* experience.

Service

As you've probably already surmised, the key is *service differentiation*—it's the *only* place where a business can break through for its customers and break out of the commodity trap. However, as we have already pointed out, mere "service" won't do the trick in today's market. This term (*service*) that numerous textbooks and business bestsellers use is simply not enough. It's Level Two. The differentiation comes at Level Three. Differentiation works . . . and differentiation is created through the *experience*.

Joe Lee, Chairman and CEO of Darden Restaurants, discussed that very concept on CNBC during an interview with Bill Griffeth.

Griffeth asked, "I am guessing the thing that could keep you up nights, though, would not be the economy itself but it would be customer boredom, you know, being tired of the menu, same old, same old. How do you combat that?"

Lee responded, "Well, one of the things that is our war cry is to keep Red Lobster and Olive Garden, our two large concepts—the secret is to keep those concepts vibrant and fresh and really meaningful to the consumers as they change their needs and desires."

If I'm in the restaurant business, I want to be Darden. Look at their lineup: Olive Garden, Red Lobster, Smokey Bones BBQ, and Bahama Breeze. It's the largest casual-dining restaurant company in the world. Darden operates more than 1,300 Red Lobster, Olive Garden, Bahama Breeze, Smokey Bones BBQ, and Seasons52 restaurants in North America. They employ more than 140,000 people. Interestingly, all of the restaurants are company owned. The company does not franchise.

Yet even a company like Darden is completely aware that it must keep the customer experience fresh. As Jim Collins wrote in the classic first line of the best seller *Good to Great*, "Good is the enemy of great." If everything is the same—it's boring!

So Much Is So Boring

Because of this phenomenon, customers have developed a sense of ennui about just about everything. Let's face it, we're much harder to impress than ever before.

Women's Wear Daily, in an article titled "Boredom on the Runways," asked the question: "Who is to blame for boredom on the runways—timid designers or bottom line-fixated retailers who are afraid to take chances in one of the world's riskiest businesses?"[4]

Kal Ruttenstein, senior vice president of fashion direction at Bloomingdale's, said in the *Women's Wear Daily* article:

> The assumption . . . is that fashion and good retail sales are at the opposite ends of the spectrum. At Bloomingdale's, fashion is what propels the business. We are fortunate enough to have customers who want excitement. We have customers who come in here weekly, if not daily, to see what has come in that is new. This is what they want, not replacement items. When our stocks get basic, our business suffers. We're very disappointed when we see only safe clothes. Safe means boring, and boring clothes don't ring cash registers, especially at the price points clothes are marked today.

Yet, isn't that what most organizations do—play it safe? And, isn't that safety the foundation of boring products and services? I believe most organizations have never taken to heart the message of Mr. Rutlensteing: safe is boring . . . and boring doesn't ring cash registers!

Let's examine three questions you can ask to begin to break away from boredom:

1. What is different about the experience of doing business with us as opposed to a competitor?

2. What programs are in place to keep employees from becoming bored?

3. How do we provide variety in our experience to prevent "loyalty fatigue" from our customers?

What is different about the experience of doing business with us as opposed to a competitor? What would it be like to do business with you? What's it like when a customer goes to your competitor? Is there a difference in the experience? If not, why should the customer do business with you? If you don't know the answer to these important questions, you are going to have to do some "detective work" to uncover important information.

Believe it or not, there is a Mystery Shopping Providers Association. I'm serious! They state on their Web site (www.mysteryshop.org) the purpose of their global association, "The MSPA is the largest professional trade association dedicated to improving service quality using anonymous resources." They even have an association "Hall of Fame" of mystery shopping, a mystery shopping certification program, and they conduct a conference to educate people on the proper techniques of mystery shopping.

According to a presentation (found on the organization's Web site) by the first president of the association, Mark Michelson, "Mystery shopping is the practice of using trained shoppers to anonymously evaluate customer service, operations, employee integrity, merchandising, and product quality." He even suggests that corporations are globally spending *a billion and a half dollars* a year on mystery shopping!

My questions for you are: Have you done any mystery shopping? Do you even know the variation between the experiences you provide your customers and what your competition is doing? If you don't know what the experience is that your rivals are providing, how do you know if your experience is unique? Remember, differentiation is of primary importance!

Naturally, your choice can be either to take a highly detailed and scientific approach, such as that suggested by the MSPA, or to just gather some information on your own. The important point is that you do something! Your dry cleaners—or major fast-food chain—had better know what the customers of your competitors are experiencing as compared and contrasted to yours. And, don't forget, unless you've created those "raving fans" we spoke of earlier, your customers and their customers are probably the same people.

No matter your choice of approach, you must be aware and sensitive to steps you can take to "tweak" your approach so that it provides a superior—and differentiated—customer experience.

You can be absolutely certain that jetBlue totally knew and understood the Southwest customer experience. I'll bet that Coffee Bean & Tea Leaf knows the specific ways in which their customers are finding a bit of differentiation between them and Starbucks.

Make a list of these specific points. Then find a way to accentuate those factors that make your approach different from your opponent in the marketplace. If you fail to understand how much these little points of differentiation matter, reflect on our earlier example of Wal-Mart and Kmart . . . and the role of the greeter at the front of the store.

What programs are in place to keep employees from becoming bored? Your employees are the delivery system for your organization's customer experience. Here's the bottom line: if they're bored, they're boring your customers.

If [your employees are] bored, they're boring your customers.

You and I have both shopped at certain stores where the employees seem to project the motto: "We're not happy until you're not happy!" Some employees are so bored—no matter what the industry or job—they are customer redirectors! Their approach is so disengaging that they motivate your customers and prospects to go elsewhere! Ask yourself and your organization this question: Do we have programs and strategies in place to make certain our employees and colleagues feel connected to our organization?

If you want to prevent customer disconnection, you need to be willing to preclude employee disconnection.

The Gallup Organization has performed fascinating studies on employee engagement.[5] They summarize the importance of the employee's emotional involvement in these three critical factors:

1. Employees who use their natural talents in their jobs are significantly more productive than average workers, both as individuals and as team members.

2. Customers recognize the commitment employees feel toward them and respond with emotion.

3. This emotion-driven reaction creates engagement, the key driver of sustainable growth and profitability.

Obviously, this begs the question, are you putting your employees in the position where they can use (and you can exploit in a positive manner) their *natural* talents? Gallup's research states that *only 20 percent* of employees say that their job gives them a chance to do what they do best.

And once you have them where their natural talent is used for the good of the organization, does each employee know what's expected?

After I graduated from Franklin College of Indiana, I was offered a job as the director of public affairs and annual fund. Basically, they had me doing two jobs at once; I was the public relations person for the college, *and* I was in charge of the campaign to raise cash gifts to the institution. Quite a combination!

I had a great deal of experience in the working world by this time—I had already had full-time jobs in selling, in radio, and in my family's grocery store. However, this was the first time I'd had a "job description."

The document outlined all the various duties of the position, as cobbled together as the responsibilities seemed to be. But it was the final point that caused the most concern: "And various duties and responsibilities as assigned by superiors." At the end of the day—and by the time I had reached the end of my rope about the job—I had spent one heck of a lot of time on those "various duties." I found myself often floundering, because I was clear about some of the tasks I was supposed to accomplish—enhancing public relations and fund-raising—yet I was in the dark about so many other things.

Gallup research shows that only about 40 percent of employees strongly agree with the simple statement "I know what is expected of me at work." Speaking from experience, if your employees don't know what's expected of them, it is difficult for them to deliver for you in a manner that engages customers.

Greg Smith, CEO of management-consulting firm Chart Your Course International, states, "Getting employees' ideas and getting their involvement is critical in our rapidly changing world. If your company is going to be competitive, it's mandatory to involve not just hands, but the ideas from everyone in your organization."[6] So most unimaginative organizations put up "idea boxes" and have "feedback programs," yet they *never take action* on the concepts presented!

Remember the adage "Behavior rewarded is behavior repeated"? Guess what happens when you don't reward ideas? You stop receiving them!

Researcher Dr. Bruce Fau discovered the surprising fact that employee surveys requesting input and ideas actually *do more harm than good* if the organization is not willing to put some of the proposals into practice! The result is that employees come to believe—rightly or wrongly—that the company couldn't care less about their input and is asking only because it is something it is "supposed" to do.

By the way, these employee-involvement efforts not only assist you in growing customers—you grow your bottom line, as well.

Aon Consulting conducted a study on employee commitment for a service organization with ten thousand employees. By taking action on the firm's ideas to reduce turnover and improve productivity, the company has reduced customer complaints, and it has found that not only has productivity improved every year for four consecutive years, but it has also decreased turnover by 11.3 percent, which is saving the organization $11.3 million annually.

Your commitment is vital—and your approach will, naturally, vary depending on your specific business. The important point is to begin now to evaluate your efforts to keep employees engaged, because they will be the ones who involve your customers. In the words of the great business philosopher W. C. Fields, "Remember, even a dead fish can float downstream, but it takes a live one to swim upstream."

How do we provide variety in our experience to prevent "loyalty fatigue" from our customers? What is "loyalty fatigue"? It's customers' growing indifference to your attempts at creating an allegiance to your business.

For example, many companies offer loyalty cards—a program that gives customers points for doing business with the company. However, a recent survey in the British publication *The Observer* reported that an astonishing 25 percent of all loyalty cardholders do not even use the points they have earned! The study said that in the United Kingdom, £413,000,000 (approximately $782 million) worth of points is going unclaimed.[7]

As a very-frequent flyer, I've often joked that I'm looking for the airline that lets me cash in forty thousand points so I can stay home!

Allyson Stewart-Allen, director of International Marketing Partners, detects signs of loyalty fatigue because of disappointment with what the loyalty schemes currently offer. According to the previously mentioned British report, Stewart-Allen said that if her usual supermarket offered her ideas on ways to cut her weekly shopping bill, or offered her a cup of coffee after her shopping, she would be more impressed.

My theory is that the initial success of one of the primary loyalty plans originated more than two decades ago—the frequent-flyer programs offered by airlines—created a perception that may not be accurate in today's marketplace. When American Airlines announced its AAdvantage program in May 1981, it was following in the long tradition of cigarette coupons and Green Stamps; in other words, retain customers through rewards. It's important to note that the great number of awards obtained by members is either free trips on the airline you are already riding extensively, or upgrades to first class on the flights you have already purchased.

This created the belief that the best way to reward your customers to create loyalty is to give them for free some of the stuff you're already selling as a prize for doing business with you. Now, in the travel business alone there are more than seventy frequent-flyer programs—involving airlines, hotels, and rental cars—all playing Follow the Leader. It seems no organization has considered the insight of customers represented by the example of Allyson Stewart-Allen. Notice, she didn't want free groceries! She wanted three primary things she considered to be rewards: education, information, and relationship building.

I wish just one airline was innovative enough to offer me, for example, a portable DVD player to watch movies as I fly when I reach a certain level of status. In other words, how about some innovation and variety?

It seems as if that is asking too much from many organizations. One airline does it a particular way, so all competitors must do the same. It's the fast-food approach—consistency is king. McDonald's often says that a Big Mac is the same Big Mac whether you buy it in Portland, Maine, or Portland, Oregon. Yet McDonald's has seen its market share eroding, and a former CEO of Burger King is quoted by Tom Peters as saying he retired because the delivery of service was pretty boring.

Here's the point: As customers, we want consistency in the Level One interactions with your organization. However, we don't want you to be so consistent that you become boring when we get to Level Three! That's not an easy thing for a business to do—emphasize consistency at one point in customer interaction, yet undermine it in the implementation of the customer experience.

The Tuck School of Business at Dartmouth University stated in a recent report, "Moving from customer satisfaction to customer loyalty is vital and very tied to customer emotions. Services can be a key to creating great customer experiences that address unarticulated needs, provide a total solution instead of just a product and generate positive customer emotions." As we study emotional involvement, it's quickly learned that constant repetition of an identical experience reduces connection and sensation about that experience. Unless you create a strategy that keeps the experience fresh, you are sowing the seeds of customer disconnection.

Here are some questions to get your thinking started:

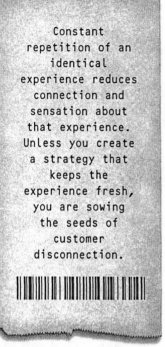

> Constant repetition of an identical experience reduces connection and sensation about that experience. Unless you create a strategy that keeps the experience fresh, you are sowing the seeds of customer disconnection.

- How is your current customer experience different from what it was a year ago?

- How much interactivity is built into the customer experience? (The higher the interactivity, the greater the variety in the experience.)

- To what degree does everything look the same as it did a year ago? Store? Materials? Web site?

- Do you have a "What's New?" section anywhere for your customers to access?

- Are there any "Limited Time Offers" that change from month to month?

- Do you communicate these new approaches and special offers to customers via unique marketing and/or e-mails?

Differentiation Strategies

To create a compelling and unique strategy, begin with a commitment to analyze your current situation. And, as you might expect from someone who was a broadcast journalist for many years, let me suggest that there are no better questions than the little ones any cub reporter is taught to ask: *Who? What? When? Where? Why? How?*

Who are your customers? Who from your organization talks to them? Whom would you like to communicate with them? Who influences them outside your organization? Whom are they with when they use your product or service?

What are customers doing with your product or service? What are they trying to accomplish? What are they experiencing by doing business with you? What are other ways they can use your product or service? What would cause the customer to change suppliers—either away from you or in your favor?

When do they decide to purchase your product or service? When do they use it? When might each be a potential for repeat business? (I once presented a program to Rogers Instruments and their division that builds magnificent church organs. Once a church buys from them, it is probably thirty to fifty years before they are in the market again. Contrast that to Coke, for example. When is their "busy season"?)

Where do they use your product or service? Where would they like to use it? Is there a way you can change the "where" of purchase to make the "where" of use more convenient? (This morning, Albertson's delivered our groceries to our door—on Sunday before church! Since they enabled the where *of purchase* to become the same as the where *of use*, we changed supermarkets from another company to Albertson's. What's that worth to their company over the next, say, decade?) Where *else* could they use your product or service?

Why do they need you in the first place? Why have they chosen you over your competitor? Why have some gone the other direction? Why would they change suppliers? Why haven't you earned their business? Why would they spend more time and money with you?

How do they use your product or service? How well are you tackling their problems and challenges? And, while we're on that word, how is the "blocking and tackling" going at your business? In other words, how is Level One processing going? (Remember, you can't move them up the steps unless you get the first one right.) How is your product financed? How well are customer and employee concerns being addressed? How fast do you respond?

To create *your* differentiation strategy, understand that the answer to *each* of these questions can create a point of differentiation and get beyond the customer disconnection of "sameness." If you want to really get results, schedule short meetings for six consecutive weeks. Each week, have your colleagues address one of the who, what, when, where, why, and how questions. Compel them to be innovative in their responses. Focus on each of these areas as a gold mine of ideas for specific strategies of differentiation.

Let's note, as well, that this exercise will work very effectively for a department or team at a large organization. However, perhaps its best use is within a small organization where there may not be considerable financial resources—and, therefore, where there is a significant need for the power of ideas and innovation.

For example, by asking this question, who are our customers?— and really searching for the answer—the aftermarket automotive filter industry was surprised to discover that there was actually a decline in the revenue generated by do-it-yourselfers (DIY). Some organizations then sought to differentiate, then changed their business to offer additional service, such as professional installation, and moved from focusing on a commodity product (an oil filter) into a value-added, compelling place to do business.

Notice, however, that these automotive shops didn't just "think outside the box"; they took specific action! It is not enough to communicate differently—you have to DO differently!

"Health care organizations (HCO's) differentiate themselves on how they *behave* differently almost as often as they do on how they are different from rivals," reports Dr. Scott MacStravic of health-care consulting firm Durable Value Marketing in an article in *Health Care Strategic Management*.

He continues:

In the Awards Yearbook, 29% of winning advertisements focused primarily or exclusively on the *events* and *experiences* that consumers can expect with the HCO. Specific experiences may be cited: "We will greet you with a smile, discuss patient needs in person, give you a free massage with your mammography," or "You will have a short wait, get test results promptly, experience little or no pain." In [this] "doing different" positioning, HCOs must recognize that different consumers, as individuals or segments, may view the same experiences differently. Some may demand prompt and efficient service, while others are willing to wait if they are treated in a friendly, caring manner. Desirable experiences may be different for individual consumers in particular situations and may change during the experience, as when expectant mothers demand natural childbirth, then change their minds when experiencing labor pain.[8]

Dr. MacStravic also makes this vitally important point: "When claiming subjective attributes such as friendliness, helpfulness, caring, comfort or other valued dimensions, the HCO must strive to ensure that its facilities and staff live up to their billing." No matter our industry, we all must do the same—we have to live up to our billing.

SWOT's Next?

Another way to prepare our organizations for creating strategies that separate us from sameness is the "SWOT" approach. (By the way, this is the American version of SWOT. In the United Kingdom, to "swot" is to cram for an exam; also, if a person *is* a "swot," it means he is something like a "nerd.") This version "comes from an old term from the strategic planning field," says Fred Wiersema, coauthor of *The Discipline of Market Leaders.* After you've focused on the six previous questions, turn your attention to SWOT:

* *Strengths*
* *Weaknesses*
* *Opportunities*
* *Threats*

It's a truly concentrated approach for cutting through the clutter and focusing on primary issues within your organization. Literally hundreds of major corporations are already using SWOT; however, this approach is one that *every* organization—no matter the size or industry—can implement to enhance its connection to customers.

An article by Stacy Collett in the July 2000 issue of *Computerworld* magazine stated that the point of SWOT is to be perfectly clear about your organization and its approaches before a strategy is implemented. "The purpose of strategy is to be really clear before you take the direction. The point of a SWOT analysis is to have the best shot at a grounded plan," Rashi Glazer, codirector of the Center for Marketing and Technology at the University of California at Berkeley, said in the article. "Clarity in strategy works. Fuzzy strategies fail. Most strategies fail because they don't have a clear direction."

If you've already held the six sessions analyzing the *who, what, when, where, why,* and *how,* it will be easy for you to do a SWOT session as well. Simply continue for four more weeks, each week having your small group focus on one of the SWOT elements. It sounds overly simple, but all you really have to do is put up notepaper or stand in front of a large blackboard and say to the group, "Let's identify our organization/department/store's most pressing strengths/weaknesses/opportunities/threats." Then, start writing. Along the way, you will find there will be a point at which there is either consensus in your group or a need to move to an important discussion regarding organizational priorities.

Be aware that SWOT certainly isn't perfect. "While useful for reducing a large quantity of situational factors into a more manageable profile, the SWOT framework has a tendency to over-simplify the situation by classifying the firm's environmental factors into categories in which they may not always fit," suggested the *New Straits Times* in April 2003. "The classification of some factors as strengths or weaknesses, or as opportunities or threats, can be seen as somewhat arbitrary. For example, the corporate culture of a company can be either a strength or a weakness. A technological change can be a threat or an opportunity."[9]

However, as the old cliché says, "Forewarned is forearmed." If you are sensitive to the imperfections of the approach, you can take steps to prevent them.

In an article in *Jewelers Circular Keystone*, Hedda Schupak relates a terrific example of SWOT:

> Consider the early part of the 20th century. At that time, America moved by rail. But the railroad companies failed to recognize that they were simply one part of a new, growing, larger entity—the transportation industry. At the same time, an ancestor of the French Hermes family recognized the automobile would replace the horse as a means of transportation. He recommended that the family firm diversify and regard their enterprise not as luxury leather saddle-makers, but as purveyors of luxury travel accoutrements.
>
> Did he do a SWOT analysis? Probably not in the formal sense. But he kept an open mind and saw that societal change would affect his business. Today, there's a two- to three-year waiting list for some Hermes bags—but you can't travel by train to most of the United States.[10]

Pulling It All Together

Leading business theorist Michael Porter—whom *Fast Company* magazine called "the world's most famous business school professor"— proposed that an organization's strengths ultimately are either (a) cost advantage, or (b) differentiation.

When a company applies their strengths—in either a wide or limited capacity—Porter suggests that three common strategies result: *differentiation, cost leadership*, and *focus*.

Porter's argument is that to attain long-term success, an organization's leadership must elect to pursue only one of these three common strategies. If they attempt more than one, the business will be (like the old hit song by Stealer's Wheel) "stuck in the middle" and will fail to achieve the competitive advantage it desires.[11]

Well, I certainly wouldn't want to quibble with such an esteemed and genuinely original thinker as Porter. However, my experience teaches me that a very small number of highly original organizations can and *do* accomplish all three—and those unique companies are the very ones that transcend comparison. They use what we've discussed to create a differentiated island in the vast ocean of commodity. They seek to ascertain—and then compellingly provide—what customers REALLY want.

The oft-discussed Southwest Airlines places its focus on its customers' needs for reasonably priced travel. Its cost-containment strategies are as good as or better than anyone else's in their industry. And we've already established that the company offers a very different style and type of product and service from their competitors.

Change the industry to sporting goods and apparel, and you could write basically the same paragraph about Nike. You could do it in other major industries—and you could also do the same exercise with highly successful local and regional businesses, as well. Think of the shoe store that holds down costs; focuses on just its local area and its uniqueness; and provides a differentiated, high-quality, and personal service that allows it to continue to compete in the world of "big-box" retailers. They're out there—big *and* small.

As you tie together your information to create a coherent strategy, you will probably choose to place a higher emphasis on one of the three common strategies than another. Porter calls organizational leaders the "guardian of trade-offs." You just can't touch *all* the bases. Yet it is my belief that the differentiated organization understands the role of paying great attention to costs—but is not a slave to the mantra of cutting costs without a consideration of the impact on customers and employees. This same organization must be highly focused—or else it fails to execute the very differentiation strategies it creates.

Armed with both the SWOT information and the insights gained about customers and your roles with them from the six questions, your goal now is to pull these two areas of information together to create *your* strategy of differentiation.

As mentioned earlier, your plan will obviously be based on your business, your customers' needs, and your ability to execute your chosen plan. And it should go without saying that you can't base your differentiation plan on the same thing someone else in your industry is doing! (That wouldn't be differentiation, now, would it?)

Here are four basic points to consider as you create your "connection through differentiation" design:

1. The goal of your strategy is to create a competitive advantage by developing—through your product and/or service—an aspect of your connection with customers that is perceived to be unique in some significant fashion.

2. The power of your differentiation strategy is in proportion to the degree of difficulty your competitors will have in duplicating your efforts.

3. Your differentiation strategy should identify specific aspects that your customers consider significant—and that they are willing to pay for. Remember, regardless of the actual value added to a product by differentiation, your customers will only invest their money in value they *perceive*.

4. Execution of a successful differentiation strategy will enable your organization to:

   • attain significant customer loyalty;

   • enhance both the number and quality of referrals from your current customer base;

   • increase the margin on the sale of your products or services;

   • increase both the number of sales and the amount of each sale per customer;

   • create a significant barrier to new competition; and

   • reduce the customer's interest in—and power over—price negotiations. Because your differentiated product or service is perceived to have added value and uniqueness, customers are less equipped to compare your offerings to your competitors.

There are mistakes, however, that organizations can make as they go through this process. Primary among these is a lack of communication throughout an organization about this important strategy. Dr. Michael Porter addressed this in his interview in the previously mentioned article in *Fast Company* when he said,

> If people in the organization don't understand how a company is supposed to be different, how it creates value compared to its rivals, then how can they possibly make all of the myriad choices they have to make? Every salesman has to know the strategy—otherwise, he won't know whom to call on. Every engineer has to understand it, or she won't know what to build.

It is absolutely mandatory that *every* person in your organization not only understands your product, but is also able to communicate how you are unique in the marketplace!

Four additional areas of potential challenge:

1. A misunderstanding or incorrect assumption as to what customers consider added value (if customers fail to value your differentiation features, then your efforts may be defeated by low-cost strategies)

2. Failure to communicate your uniqueness to customers, therefore preventing them from perceiving the added value in your differentiation

3. Overdoing it—being so differentiated that the cost of production requires that you charge a price that customers resist

4. Creating aspects that are easily copied by competitors, therefore producing no sustainable competitive advantage

At the end of the day, the effort you make to close the disconnect between the generic, bland approach of most organizations and the uniqueness that customers seek will be worth all of your time and trouble.

Think of it this way (to continue the personal romance analogy of previous chapters): if every man was the same, why would you pick the specific one you did to be your husband or partner? If every woman was the same, why is the one you're with your significant other or your wife? My bet is that there is something—some quality, some trait, some aspect—to the person you are in love with that differentiated him or her from everyone else you ever dated. That uniqueness is what propelled many of us headlong into love!

As life progresses, our hope is to celebrate and venerate that important and singular aspect. In fact, for a huge number of us, that differentiation is so compelling that we made a highly significant, highly personal commitment to that other individual.

If we realize that uniqueness is so powerful that it can draw us into making a lifetime commitment on a personal basis, why wouldn't we move heaven and earth to follow that example with customers? Why don't we try to create a special feeling for and about them that may create a commitment and loyalty on their part that will benefit us for years to come? Ironic, isn't it? These same steps that benefit our organizations so highly also provide customers with what they REALLY want.

Executive Summary

The Fourth Disconnection is that what customers REALLY want is differentiation—however, most organizations offer sameness and, therefore, boredom.

- There is power in differentiation.
  - Too often, everything looks the same from the customer's perspective.
  - Sooner or later, every industry—and therefore every business—will face the pressure of commoditization. However, EVERY product or service can find a strategy that will transcend commodity.
  - Commodity is based upon three aspects—and each aspect has its own challenges:

    Price: If all I focus upon is being the cheapest, then all you have to do is make your product or service cheaper and you defeat me. Therefore, companies such as Home Depot and Sony have simply decided it is not in their—nor their customer's—interest to play that game. Certainly price is important; however, if it was the only factor, Kmart would not have suffered bankruptcy as Wal-Mart became America's biggest corporation.

Quality: The problem with quality is that it is always subjective. Most organizations hear the word *quality* and focus upon their product manufacturing or their service delivery. Yet, companies must also enhance the quality of their customer relationships to transcend the commodity trap.

Service: Enhancing service is thought to be a major strategy for breaking out of the commodity trap. However, as we have already clearly seen, your organization MUST define service in the same manner as your customer and then seek to expand your execution to deliver not just exemplary service, but also a compelling customer experience.

- A major challenge any organization must face in dealing with its best clients is the potential for customer boredom.
  - To assist in preventing this, ask yourself and your colleagues these three important questions:

    What is different about the experience of doing business with us as opposed to a competitor?

    What programs are in place to prevent frontline employees from becoming bored and thereby creating bored or unengaged customers?

    How do we provide variety in our experience to prevent "loyalty fatigue" from our customers?
- The ongoing challenge of differentiation is a difficult one for any organization.

○ To begin the process of strategic differentiation, simply work from the six basic questions that any first-year journalism student is taught:

- Who? What? When? Where? Why? How?
  - Who is providing the differentiated experience? What is that experience? When is our organization providing it? Where does it take place for our customers? Why is it creating differentiation at the grassroots level? How can we expand on that differentiation to create greater uniqueness for our product or service in the mind of the customer?
- Take the information gleaned from these questions and perform a SWOT analysis for your organization: *strengths, weaknesses, opportunities, threats.*

Then, use this information to create a compelling strategy of differentiation.

○ The power of the strategy you develop will encourage differentiation proportionate to the degree of difficulty it provides for your competitors to duplicate.

○ Focus upon your customers' perception of differentiation and added value. Therefore, you are only identifying aspects and creating product and service strategies that they find valuable and are willing to pay for.

○ Set an organizational goal to create a competitive advantage through differentiation and reap the benefits of executing those strategies.

○ Thoroughly educate your colleagues so that there is uniformity in the embracing of the importance of differentiation and understanding of the strategies and programs to achieve that organizational goal.

Bridge Building
Moving from Sameness to Differentiation

- Do you consider—or perhaps the best way to ask the question is *did* you consider before reading the preceding chapter—your products or services to be a commodity?

- Examine how the three aspects of commodity come into play for your organization. How does your organization stack up against the competition on these three fronts? Is there a compelling differentiation in any of the areas? Remember, they are:
  - Price
  - Quality
  - Service

- Let's repeat three questions asked in the chapter . . . and be certain to write down your answers and encourage your colleagues to do the same:
  - What is different about the experience of doing business with us as opposed to a competitor?
  - What programs are in place to keep employees from becoming bored?
  - How do we provide variety in our experience to prevent our customers from having "loyalty fatigue"?

- How have you used mystery shopping to reveal points of differentiation between you and your competition?

- Have you held SWOT sessions?

- Take a look at the three areas defined by Michael Porter regarding organizational strengths:
  - Differentiation
  - Cost leadership
  - Focus

- Now ask yourself these questions and encourage your colleagues to do the same:
  - How has your organization traditionally been regarding these three strengths? How about your competition?
  - What do you need to do to create a CCA to enhance client loyalty and to increase your customer base?
  - Can you do more than one? Should you?

5

THE FIFTH DISCONNECTION

What Customers REALLY Want: *Coordination*
What Business Offers: *Confusion*

The headline of the article in the March 22, 2004, edition of the *Wall Street Journal* stated the case well: "When One Hand Doesn't Know What the Other Hand is Doing, Customers Notice. And They Aren't Pleased."

More customers now are more confused than ever. Customers are baffled when one segment of your organization tells them one thing— and another department informs them another. They're perplexed when they realize they're confronted with a plethora of choices. And, of greatest concern for your company, they're exiting from their relationships with you to do business with an easier-to-deal-with organization.

When we spend most of our time working within our organizations, we can readily defend why we're structured in the manner we are. We understand why one telephone line takes care of one situation—and another handles a different issue. We know why something is a "company policy" to which we should hold fast.

Problem is . . . our customers *don't*.

One of the interesting points I discovered when talking with friends and associates about this chapter was that *every* single person had some story to tell me about customer confusion. Some joked that it almost seemed as though companies were working three shifts to engineer a new process to make the maze of business more confusing for their customers. They smiled and said it appeared as if companies decided they didn't want the bored customers of the previous chapter—so they decided to create frustrated ones!

OK, I Have a Story Too!

When I moved to Las Vegas a couple of years ago, I discovered that Sprint is the local telephone provider. *Great!* I thought. *Now I will be able to have one bill for my local, long-distance, and cellular accounts.* Convenient, right? Of course. Possible, right? Of course *not*.

"Sorry, sir. That's a separate division of Sprint. You'll have to contact them directly regarding mobile telephone service," an employee explained.

"So, in other words," I asked, "you're content with me staying with another provider because you can't simplify my life in this manner?"

"I guess so, sir," was the response.

Why would an organization take the risk of losing a customer simply because that client did business with more than one area of the company and therefore wanted coordination? Even if all Sprint did was to transfer my call to the PCS mobile area, I would've been reasonably happy. But what I really wanted them to do was make my life simpler—and instead, there was no reduction in my effort and a greater chance I was going to end up frustrated and confused.

Many big corporations have focused extensively on maximizing efforts within sales channels. However, what they have often failed to consider is that today's customers will access products and services through *multiple* channels—and expect a company to have its act together to recognize their need for coordination.

If I purchase a product online, I want to be able to return it at your local store. If I order it online, and you have a local store, I want to be able to come in and pick it up right away at your location. (It should be obvious that this is good for your organization—according to a Sears study, 21 percent of customers will buy additional products when they come in to pick up the item they've ordered online![1])

Yet so many times, instead of coordination of sales channels, customers are met by confusion.

Those "Dumb" Customers

I don't believe for a moment that "the customer is always right." Sometimes they're wrong, sometimes they're impolite, and sometimes they are just plain stupid. If you want proof that maxim is wrong, just check out this Web site: www.CustomersSuck.com. There you will see what service employees are saying about the people they serve. On the discussion board

The customer is
not always right
. . .
but he's *still*
the customer!

there, I've read stories about everything from customers who say stupid things, to the just plain mean people that our frontline folks sometimes encounter. Here are a few (slightly edited for propriety and punctuation; used by permission) examples from the site:

- "*I was putting movies away, constantly keeping an eye on the counter for customers. The second I see someone, I will drop what I am doing and help them. One idiot decided to find me first and shouted, 'Hey, get to the counter, I'm ready!'*"

- Customer: *I need to see if you show that my check from you went through the bank & turned into money.*

  CSR: *You need to see if it's been cashed?*

  CUSTOMER: *Well, I need to know if it's gotten sent through the bank & turned into money.*

  CSR: *So . . . you need to see if it's been CASHED?*

  CUSTOMER: *Uh . . . well, I need to know if it has been turned into money. So not really cashed, no . . .*

- *"'Well you used to . . .' If I had a dollar for every time some moron came in and said that, I'd make Bill Gates look broke. Are they trying to tell me something that I don't already know when they say that? Yes people, I know we used to have a catalog and have car audio [crud] and so on and so forth, but we don't anymore. This lady came in today and wanted an alarm clock that we stopped carrying and started going off on me on how we used to carry them. I KNOW WE DID BUT WE DO NOT HAVE IT ANYMORE!!!!! I mean, do you go to a Honda Dealership and ask them if they have any Preludes? And when they say no, do you respond, 'Well, you used to . . .'"*

- *"From ABC News: Wal-Mart workers called deputies after a blood-soaked man walked into the store and bought some clothes, bandages and trash bags around 4 a.m. He paid with a $100 bill that also appeared to be bloodstained, they said, and drove off in a pickup. (I don't think we need Sherlock Holmes for this one.)"*

Sure, customers do and say dumb things. They irritate us—even in some cases make us angry. Yet, even though they are not always right—they are always the *customers*! Therefore, we may have reasons to get upset with them, but these reasons *cannot* become excuses for anything less than a compelling performance for them on behalf of our organization. Let's examine just some of the reasons that customers can become confused. Then, we'll take a look at some of the steps organizations can take to coordinate efforts to eliminate that form of customer disconnection.

As we discuss these areas, please remember this important point: *You cannot build loyalty with a consistently confused customer.* It's impossible. Sure, you can create a loyal relationship with a *formerly* confused customer that you've assisted in her development of understanding. But if she's persistently perplexed, she is also continuing to seek other suppliers.

Confusion Generated by Competitors

Obviously, there are as many reasons customers could be confused as there are customers. Improper communication, inadequate experience with the product, a discrepancy between the experience the customer expects and what is actually delivered, and more can create uncertainty.

You cannot build loyalty with a consistently confused customer.

Unfortunately, in some cases the confusion is caused by information spread about you by your competitors. Every once in a while, you will see a strange story in a publication (ranging from the *Wall Street Journal* to the *National Enquirer*) about a business that is intentionally attempting to gain in the marketplace by creating confusion, then preying on the poor customers who can't figure it out. Whether it's an adult bookstore in Kentucky calling itself "Victoria's Secret" or a salesperson from a competitor telling prospects so-called "facts" about your product or service that just aren't true, the hard reality of the matter is that sometimes we do not create the disconnection that impacts our customers.

Some organizations have been very good at running down their competition—and many of us have encountered those women or men who "sell" by offering unsubstantiated critiques of their competitors' products and, in many cases, just flat out lying to win business. (I refuse to use the word *salesperson* here, because that term implies a professionalism that these individuals do not display.)

Perhaps the best example of this on a large scale is the political candidate who feels he can win by misrepresenting the views of his opponent. By intentionally deceiving the public regarding the opponent's real positions on the issues and promises to the electorate, this candidate sets himself up to "kill two birds with one stone" by staking out more populist ground for himself, while putting the opponent on the defensive to comment on positions that were never held. The *Washington Monthly,* back in May 1990, had an article written by Daniel Slocum Hinerfeld that addressed this issue with the very telling title: "How Political Ads Subtract: It's not the negative ones that are perverting democracy. It's the deceptive ones." The article asks the question, "Who's responsible for these misleading ads?"

The report continues:

> Sidney Galanty, the successful producer of several Democratic political campaigns and of Jane Fonda exercise videos, sounds the same note as other consultants: "The people who are causing the most problems in this country are people like me," he says. "I know how to play on people's emotions. That's what I do for a living." "Truth in advertising and accuracy in advertising sound like they're the same idea, but they're really not," says Jonathan Alter, a media and politics reporter for Newsweek.

Part of the reason this analogy is so instructive for business is found in Mr. Galanty's insights. To achieve his goal of deception, he plays on "people's *emotions*." However, what do most organizations do when confronted with this type of problem competitor? They attempt to respond with *evidence* to prove their case. That's not a bad idea; however, notice how the facts pale in persuasive power to emotion.

Remember the advertisement in the presidential election of 1988 when Michael Dukakis was blasted for his stand on the environment by then Vice President Bush? If not, here is the script for the "Bush for President" advertisement:

> As a candidate, Michael Dukakis called Boston Harbor an open sewer. As governor he had the opportunity to do something about it but chose not to. The Environmental Protection Agency called his lack of action the most expensive public policy mistake in the history of New England. Now Boston Harbor, the dirtiest harbor in America, will cost residents $6 billion to clean. And Michael Dukakis promises to do for America what he's done for Massachusetts.

The article from *Washington Monthly* continues:

The facts of the harbor ad, all technically accurate, were also carefully selected. As [*Newsweek*'s Jonathan] Alter points out, "They neglect to mention two points that are so important that they make the ad fundamentally untruthful." Those points? That Dukakis was the first Massachusetts governor to try to clean up the harbor, and that the Reagan-Bush administration blocked his efforts. The ad gave the sense that Bush had a stronger environmental record, which, as Alter says, "was simply a deeply misleading notion to convey to the voting public."

Yet, the article fails to critique the biggest part of the problem: Dukakis's response—or lack thereof. When the Massachusetts governor used facts and figures in retaliation for the "Harbor" ad by the Bush campaign, the voting public tuned him out. Bush's campaign had created an emotional connection—Dukakis's strategy for explaining was an intellectual one. We remember which candidate achieved victory in the marketplace of the public.

The purpose of this point is not to engage in a political discussion in any manner; it is to use an example that most of us will remember to illustrate the importance of this point: If your competitor is confusing the marketplace by using deception, you need to answer first with a response engineered toward the emotion of your customers and prospects.

In his book *My Life*, former president Bill Clinton describes the time that his opponent in a race for governor of Arkansas created a similarly deceptive advertisement against Clinton. Mr. Clinton's response was to go on the air with a television ad of his own, saying of his opponent's attack, "If he won't tell you the truth in the campaign, how in the world do you expect him to tell the truth if he's in office?" Checkmate.

Clinton did not respond at first with evidence—he appealed to the Arkansas voter's gut reaction that "once a liar, always a liar." (Now, I could make some comment at this point about how ironic life and politics are; however, as I said earlier, this is a discussion about business, not government or candidates.)

Of *course*, you will have to—and *want* to—also respond with the evidence that proves the competition is willfully attempting to mislead the very people to whom they hope to sell. But if you back yourself into the corner of fighting your battle by "explaining through evidence" against an emotionally charged argument, you have already lost half the battle.

Certainly, there will be many in business that will regard my position here with contempt. Many will firmly believe that the only proper way to respond to confusion and misrepresentation is with a plethora of well-researched data and analyses. I understand why they may feel that way; however, as Sigal Barsade wrote in *Administrative Science Quarterly*:

> One . . . needs to take into account the sharing of emotions, or emotional contagion, that occurs in groups. The importance of emotions in organizational behavior, particularly at the individual level, has been solidly established. The results of this research confirm that people do not live on emotional islands but, rather, that group members experience moods at work, these moods ripple out and, in the process, influence not only other group members' emotions but their group dynamics and individual cognitions, attitudes, and behaviors as well. Thus, emotional contagion, through its direct and indirect influence on employees' and work teams' emotions, judgments, and behaviors, can lead to subtle but important ripple effects in groups and organizations.[2]

It's not difficult at all to make the intellectual leap from the importance of internal emotional contagion in your employees to how vital it is to build emotional momentum with your customers and prospects.

Customer Confusion We Unintentionally Generate

When you study the areas creating the greatest amount of disorientation across the board, you will find that in most cases, we're creating more problems for ourselves than our competitors are. When you examine the customer confusion permeating the marketplace, a few prime targets become apparent:

- An overwhelming number of choices

- Incongruence between promotion and practice

- Technology vs. human touch

- Inability to execute at Level One creating disconnection at higher levels

- Technical communication presented to a nontechnical audience

Overwhelming number of choices

So you want to take a trip? Let's assume you've decided where you want to go. Now you have to decide where you want to purchase the ticket.

Why not online? There's a myriad of commercials from Expedia.com and Orbitz—as well as from each airline—attempting to get you to use the Internet to purchase your travel from them. The number of options presented on each of the sites is simply awe inspiring. So, naturally, you check several. That's too bad for the airlines that—like any business—should want to foster loyal customers. A 2002 study by Nielsen/NetRatings said that more than one-fourth of American Airlines' online users (AA.com) visited Continental.com, and about one-fifth also checked out Delta.com. This trend also applies within the realm of the large general travel sites, as one-third of Expedia's visitors clicked their Web browsers to see what Travelocity.com was offering.

Consider what our hot travel prospect encountered when she arrived at the site. "A quick vacation package search on Expedia yields over 621 options, a simple hotel search on Hotels.com produces more than 120 hotel listings and a cruise search on Cruise411.com returns over 300 cruises," says Rob Roberts, founder and CEO of Vacation Coach, Inc.[3] In other words, we end up with a significant amount of information—and practically zero wisdom.

Next, try to imagine how many fares the airlines have on any particular route. I ran a search for a round-trip ticket from Los Angeles' LAX to New York's LaGuardia and discovered that I could fly it for $265 on Frontier (if I was willing to endure a long layover), or I could be a loyal United customer for $355. Neither of these fares is outrageous by any stretch of the imagination for a thirty-day-advance, Saturday-night-stay-over, one-stop-with-a-change-of-plane, nonrefundable ticket. However, between those two airlines and others that would fly me on that trip within that price range, there were 193 different options to choose from! If you're willing to pay up to $791, you increase the number of options to more than 500!

On the other hand, if you want to go nonstop to New York City—and you are a United customer—you'll need to go into JFK instead of LaGuardia. United offers six flights on this route every day. If you want to go one way, one month from now in coach, I found a fare of $309.10. If tomorrow is your travel date, and you are a first-class flyer, a seat on that same flight will take $2,118.70—and remember, that's *one way*! (And we haven't started looking for a hotel and rental car!)

The travel industry provides a great example of confusion generated by too many choices. If you aren't a frequent traveler, how could you not read this and shake your head? Don't forget, none of this even began to cover the quality of service and the level of compelling experience a passenger could expect. (And it also left me wondering how much experiential difference there is between the $265 round trip and the $2,118 one-way.) As of this writing, Delta Airlines had just announced "SimpliFares," removing many of its restrictions—and confusion—from its airfares. The early response has been very positive and has generated additional business and enthusiasm for Delta.

We all realize that our economic system is founded on the consumer having a variety of choices. Yet we need to examine what happens when our customers have so many options that we have, inadvertently, created "paralysis by analysis."

Home Accents Today recently told the story of Eva Jeanbart-Lorenzotti, who founded her successful company, Vivre, eight years ago by selling luxury brands via an online magazine and Internet site. "Vivre is about tradition, the unique, the artisan quality and the fun of shopping," Jeanbart-Lorenzotti said. "Luxury today is more about a personal fulfillment." The article reveals her powerful and interesting philosophy about retail: "'Too many choices confuse the consumer,' she says, 'and retailers' roles are to *edit the selection* and give that shopper a reason, *besides product*, to come into their store or Web site'"[4] (emphasis added).

In other words, limit confusion between you and your customers by limiting and refining the choices you present to them. Then, leverage their positive experiences into the first step of true relationship building.

Incongruence between promotion and practice

Once again, it is worth asking—does your organization "walk its talk"? In other words, are the actions that customers experience congruent with the advertising they've read, viewed, and heard? It's so obvious—if what I experience when I do business with you is inferior to what you've led me to believe I can expect, you now have a huge credibility problem with me.

We are constantly "sweating" this in our companies with Obsidian—we're obsessed with congruency. When Pyramid Coach tells you we're superior in customer experiences in our industry, we realize the bus had better not break down. *And* the driver had better have an engaging personality, as well as a commitment to client satisfaction on a 24/7 basis. Anything less, and we have not lived up to our end of the bargain. As I mentioned earlier, some of us at Obsidian have joked about the title of that best-selling self-help book called *Don't Sweat the Small Stuff.* We've decided that—at least in our companies—there is *no small stuff!* You know as well as we do that this is true because—to quote a crazy saying—"little fires not extinguished

> Limit confusion between you and your customers by limiting and refining the choices you present to them.

> Does your organization "walk its talk"? Are the actions that customers experience congruent with the advertising they've read, viewed, and heard?

by sweat become big fires extinguished by tears." A problem is *never* easier to resolve than in the moments when it appears small. We sweat the details. How else can we stay congruent and not confuse the customers we seek to serve?

In the field of customer communication at the sales level, the move toward team selling has created an entire new realm of potential congruency conflicts. Drs. Andrea Dixon, Julie Gassenheimer, and Terri Feldman Barr, writing in the *Journal of Personal Selling and Sales Management,* address the issue:

> Today's sales representatives face escalating competition and turbulence, increasing product proliferation, and mounting pressures to meet organizational goals and customer demands. Changes in customer contact patterns, customer expectations, and electronic customer interfaces require that sales representatives organize and effectively respond to information coming from diverse directions. With sales teams comes incongruence between individual and teamwork values or styles, creating situations in which conflict is inevitable.[5]

The authors also note in the article that the very nature of communication between an individual sales representative and core selling teams can be different. "Sales rep responses to conflict may thwart sales force efforts, attitudes, and behaviors, eventually damaging long-term relationships with customers," they state. "Since core selling teams operate on a longer-term, strategic basis, the conflict response process in this team environment plays a critical role in ensuring that the team achieves the team's objectives, has positive intra-team interactions, and builds long-term customer relationships."

As an aside, consider the challenge inherent when a sales representative—who may have been taught the "ABC" approach discussed in an earlier chapter—becomes a part of a core selling team. The team may perceive this sales rep to be much too "pushy," while the rep views the team with disdain because of the slower pace at which they move the process along. Now, imagine where the poor customer is in this process—feeling somewhat like Olive Oyl in the old *Popeye* cartoons—a sales rep pulling on one arm, attempting to "close," and a selling team patting the hand on the other arm, encouraging her to take her time and focusing on relationship building! The easiest step for the customer to take is to move on! As a customer, why not find someplace where the messages and the approaches are congruent?

It's important to note as well that conflict in and of itself does not create a congruency problem. *How* we handle the conflict is very telling to the customer. If the challenge is resolved in a manner that creates positive feelings and develops enhanced emotional connections, the conflict can actually improve the relationship. (I *don't* recommend, however, that you go out and *create* customer conflict just so you can attempt to be a "knight in shining armor." That's much too risky—and unethical!) But if the handling of the conflict is marred by missed deadlines, lack of follow-up, inadequate communication, and other actions that suggest to the customer you talk a good game, but aren't really committed to the steps that cement a relationship, then the same conflict that bonded the customer to you in the first example repels him in this one.

This is not an area of focus simply for the sales and marketing team. At *all* levels of the company, there must be significant congruence—and, as most things do, it starts at the top. Whether you are the CEO of your own one-person shop or General Electric, the demonstration that your actions are congruent with your values will be transmitted throughout your organization to your employees and your customers. If you value the human assets of your organization, you must value the importance of congruency and the volumes it speaks about what's really important. WorldCom and Enron examples have been cited ad nauseam, but they bear repeating. Do you think Ken Lay or Bernie Ebbers projected (and demanded from their colleagues) a customer-focused sense of values and a commitment to ethical congruency? Me neither.

"Congruency of values, and of the actions born from them in the daily execution of corporate strategy, is the essence of the human-assets approach," wrote Charles M. Farkas of Bain and Company and Suzy Wetlaufer of Harvard in the *Harvard Business Review* in 1996. They said:

This authority to act is awarded only to employees who already conform to the company's way of doing things. But in organizations led by effective human-assets CEOs, this group of proven team players is often large. Consider what happened at Southwest Airlines when Midway Airlines went out of business in 1991. Within hours of Midway's announcement, Southwest employees from Dallas had physically taken over every Midway gate at the Chicago airport. "I didn't even know they were going to Chicago when they left. They didn't call me first," Kelleher recalls. "They came in later and said, "Hey, Chief, we just did something; we thought you might like to know about it." They never doubted his approval, Kelleher notes, because "we have such a great congruency among our people."[6]

Picture yourself in Kellener's shoes: How would you react if your colleagues came into your office and said, "Hey, Boss! We just took over Chicago, OK?" Would they—as then-Southwest CEO Kelleher says—have never doubted your approval because they knew they were acting for customers with a congruency that was evident throughout the organization?

One of my best friends, Fred McClure, worked in both the Ronald Reagan and the George H. W. Bush administrations. When I asked Fred about the difference in working for these two leaders, his response was an interesting commentary on the importance of congruency. "While President Bush was—and is—a wonderful and compassionate man, it was in some ways easier to work for President Reagan. With Mr. Reagan, his values were so well established and communicated—and you just knew they weren't going to change—it was very easy for all of the staff to know exactly what he would want us to do. So, we didn't have to be asking for permission to do things—we just asked ourselves what the president would want us to do, and in the vast majority of cases, you just knew."

This isn't about the particular politics of the individuals; however, it is an interesting observation of different approaches to being a chief executive, even if the entity of which you're CEO is the United States of America.

How important is this? In the hotel industry, according to *Hotels* magazine, "A dramatically different model for managing customer interactions can transform customer contact operations, deliver the right customer service while developing more useful customer insight, drive out operating costs and decrease expenses by 10% to 30%."[7] And the first value to model is *congruency* between what you articulate to the customers and the actions you take on their behalf.

Technology vs. Human Touch

More than any other point in this chapter, when I would discuss this issue with friends and colleagues, the challenge of "technology vs. the human touch" would create the most passionate and visceral reactions. We're fed up with being in "voice-mail jail"; with not being able to get a real, live human being on the phone; with automated *everything*. As customers we desire the human touch! Relationships are built on human interaction—and these emotional connections are what customers REALLY want.

But you've already discovered that. So, have *you* turned off *your* voice mail? Me neither. I'm thankful for caller ID so I don't have to personally answer all those calls I want to shuttle off to my answering device. I couldn't live without e-mail—including my nice auto responder to immediately tell you when I'm away. It is so much quicker than actually communicating with someone! In other words, I want *you* to give *me* the human touch. On the other hand—like most hassled professionals—I believe that I'm too busy to give up my technology to take the time to have more personal contact with others.

A huge problem that should be keeping customer relationship managers awake at night in many organizations is finding the proper mix of the efficiency of technology in both time and money—balanced with the desire of customers to receive personal attention from a human being. "The more we become high tech, the more we desire high touch"—that insightful phrase has been around for over two decades, since John Nesbitt said it in the classic work *Megatrends* (Warner Books, 1982).

In London's *Independent Sunday*, Roger Trapp addressed this global challenge. He wrote:

We British are a patient lot. But things are changing. Gather a few people together and sooner or later, you will hear complaints. About how they were late for a dinner engagement because they had to wait in for a parcel that never came, or about how their car was not ready from its service by the time the garage said it would be. Nor is it just a British issue. In the United States, for so long considered the home of customer service, there is a growing backlash against the seeming indifference of large corporations to their customers. As companies get bigger, they must work harder to stay closer to their customers. And many are clearly relying on technology to do the job for them. This is a mistake—for at least two reasons. First, because many of the benefits of customer relationship marketing (CRM) systems are oversold; second, because these failings can be so obvious that customers realize when a company is communicating with them as part of a "market sector" rather than as the individual they say they are.[8]

A *Washington Post* article addressed the issue this way: "Customer service has deteriorated into a new kind of [technological] purgatory, one in which companies pass the buck, frequently from one corporate division to another. Or customer service representatives pin the blame on other companies. Or, even worse, they fault their customers."[9]

This issue cuts across all industries. Bank executives, for example, learned about this issue in *Bank Marketing* magazine, when Robert Hall of Xchange wrote:

> Efficiency, consistency and rules often war with the personalization customers expect and employees wish to deliver. As a result, many organizations are quickly moving to shrink the physical and psychological distance between their customers and their decisions about them. Behind Schwab's commitment to bricks is a stark fact: Branches account for 70 percent of their new customers. Wells Fargo is already seeing success, as decentralization—starting from the top and working its way to the teller line—has already produced tangible differences in Wells Fargo's California operations.[10]

Obviously, there is no hard-and-fast formula that will allow any manager to know the exact point at which speed of technology and the warmer feeling of dealing with a real person intersect to the advantage of both the customer and the organization. However, as the Roger Trapp article summarizes, every organization will "need to remember that technology is fine for running certain routine aspects of their businesses, but it is no substitute for properly motivated employees able to make appropriate decisions on behalf of customers. In the digital age, perhaps more than in any previous era, the human touch is vital."

Inability to Execute at Level One Creates Disconnection at Higher Levels

If you can't get my monthly statement correct, how in the world can I ever believe that you're hitting all the other targets customers need? If customers' attention is focused on correcting your mistakes, it is extraordinarily difficult—practically impossible—for your organization to move them to the level of customer experience that is the genesis of lifelong loyalty.

As the old cliché states, "The devil is in the details." If you cannot create a flawless product and process the customer perfectly, you'll never move up to Levels Two and Three. When *Fortune* magazine writer Janet Guyon interviewed the CEO of fashion trendsetter Prada, Patrizio Bertelli for the October 2001 issue, she received an earful on the importance of "sweating the small stuff."

"A fashion company is no different from an electronics or a car company," said Bertelli. "Like General Motors, we have to have production and manufacturing stability. Am I volatile? If a demanding manager behaving consistently is described as volatile—well, then that is the outside world's problem." Bertelli not only has the Prada brand, but he's also acquired Fendi, Jil Sander, and Helmut Lang as well. *Fortune* reports:

His goal: to reach $5 billion in sales by 2010—thereby taking on the world's two biggest luxury-goods conglomerates, LVMH and Gucci.

"I am demanding," he says. "I expect consistency and correct behavior. But I don't expect people to be perfect. I might appear harsh, but as CEO I don't flatter my ego. I have to oversee 7,500 employees. My behavior is aimed at giving them security of management to protect them." He points out that more than 150 people have worked for him for over 20 years.

If Prada achieves Bertelli's goals, it will undoubtedly happen because the amazing experience that Prada customers enjoy from the product is supported by a drive to focus on the details of Level One from the top.

Start now in your organization to reconfirm that the details—the basic blocking and tackling that isn't glamorous, yet *is* vital—is being processed with speed and accuracy so the ground is prepared for more fertile customer relationships.

Technical Communication Presented to Nontechnical Audience

In *ALL Business Is Show Business*, I explained the "Three Act" tradition of storytelling. In act one, both characters and a conflict are introduced. If the characters engage the audience, the audience will naturally want to see how they resolve the conflict in which they find themselves. Act two is the longest of the three acts, and it is all the varied attempts by the characters to resolve their conflict. Act three is where it comes together with the heroic resolution of the conflict by the characters. Most major works, from Homer's *Odyssey* to Bruce Willis's *Die Hard* have followed that formula—and isn't *that* a wide spectrum of drama?

However, there is an additional—and more difficult—aspect of communication that is more important in today's world than ever before. What happens when technical experts have to describe their products and services to prospects and clients who do not have their technical grounding? Unfortunately, in most situations the result is the disconnection between coordination and confusion we're examining here.

A few years back, I was asked to address the nuclear scientists and engineers of GE on this very matter. As I entered the auditorium, the thought that popped into my mind was, *I've never seen so many shirt pockets with plastic pen protectors in one place in my life!* These were amazingly brilliant men and women—yet the problem they were facing was exceedingly basic: How could they communicate nuclear science and energy to regular people?

If you really stop to think about it, in one way or another, there are technical aspects to whatever we do. Certainly, your work may appear to be less complex than nuclear power, yet your terminology and specifics are just as remote to those outside your industry as external specialties seem to you.

So isn't it somewhat ironic that perhaps the best advice on how to communicate technical information to nontechnical prospects, employees, and customers is centuries old? When Aristotle wrote of rhetoric, he described the steps that one should take to be persuasive in communication. These very steps are precisely the strategy we need to apply today.

Aristotle said there were three principle approaches (or means) to persuasion in speech:

1. *Ethos*: an appeal based on the character and credibility of the presenter

2. *Logos*: an appeal through the argument of the apparent truth of the matter being presented

3. *Pathos*: an appeal to the emotions of the audience

The fundamental problem most often encountered when attempting to communicate technical information regarding your product or service to a nontechnical listener is that most technical professionals assume *logos* is the approach that will be most persuasive. However, there is an inherent conflict. Because the technical speaker presumably understands the logic much better than her audience does, the detailed reasoning is often not followed by the listener, who is unable to fully comprehend the precise argument being presented. In addition, many communication experts suggest that the personalities and communication styles of those most adept at highly technical occupations tend to be centered more in dispassionate logic than in emotion or striving for personal credibility. These people presume that if the facts are outlined, the audience will reach the *same logical conclusion as the speaker* presenting the material. The disconnection is obvious—many professionals have a communication style grounded in their individual credibility and/or emotional content. For example, while some who are listening to a presidential debate regarding funding for the Star Wars missile project may be swayed by the personal credibility of the candidate, others will respond to an emotional appeal directed toward the safety of the world's people. For still others, the only thesis that will carry any weight is a scientific discussion of the feasibility of the project. No single approach will be persuasive to all. Since most of the scientists working on the project will probably tend to focus on *logos*, those individuals who respond to *ethos* and *pathos* find their highly intellectual and logical arguments unconvincing.

If you're communicating technical information to a customer base, to avoid the disconnection so often found, focus on the *ethos* and *pathos* of your communication. Since technical people tend to gravitate toward *logos*, you'll probably have that area well covered already. Consider how you can enhance personal credibility and engage emotion.

It's also worth mentioning that this disconnection is an example in miniature of why the overall challenge of customer communication is so difficult. Since most of us focus on the technical and logical nature of our product and service, we unintentionally ignore the approaches that will motivate customers to benefit from our work—*ethos* and *pathos*.

Interestingly, some text on the subject even assumes that—as was written by Keith Wegner, president of Quantalex, Inc. (a consulting group who writes technical proposals for their clients) in the trade journal *Technical Communication*—"Pathos or emotional appeal seems out of place in technical writing." This to me is akin to the old saying that I previously mentioned: "If your only tool is a hammer, every problem becomes a nail."[11] In other words, if *logos* is all you have experience in communicating, *pathos* will seem uncomfortable.

So what style should you use when communicating technical information?

1. Whatever style is most persuasive to the listener

2. Whatever works to resolve the disconnection with customers

As Cheryl and Peter Reinhold write in the journal *Solutions*, a technical communicator making a presentation "can take it as given that the interests of your nontechnical audience will *always* be different from yours."[12]

They suggest that when you understand this important concept,

instead of "What am I going to tell them about this?" you will ask, "What would they want to know about it?" Often, the "educational" approach springs from an urge to impress: "Look how complex this stuff is I'm doing." Will it win you admiration? Try *resentment* instead—plus a warning from your boss to keep things simple next time! Avoiding the "Detail Trap" and the "Logic Trap" will help you find a message the audience cares about.

Solving the Confusion Dilemma

Obviously, the best way to solve the disconnection with your customers created by confusion is to not allow it to happen in the first place. This requires emotional connections with your customers. However, since many managers are typically aggressive, mistakes are often made in communication that are—to use a tennis term—an "unforced error." You don't mean to confuse the customer; however, the often-forceful nature of business today creates the climate where the aforementioned disconnections are easily, if unintentionally, created.

USA Today explored the similarity of management and tennis in an article titled "CEOs Take a Lesson from Tennis," written by Del Jones in July 2004:

Last year in the men's singles matches at Wimbledon, players who made the fewest unforced errors won 70% of the time, according to an analysis done for *USA Today* by IBM tennis consultant Keith Sohl of London. In the 127 matches, the losers had 706 more unforced errors than the winners. Perhaps more telling, in the final 31 matches, when the world's best played each other, the percentage of unforced errors dropped dramatically among both winning and losing players. Even so, the winners had the least unforced errors even *more* often, 74% of the time in those final matches.

What constitutes an "unforced error" in business? According to *USA Today*, "Most seem minor and occur day to day. 'I can't tell you how angry business customers get when the vendor can't get a bill to them on time or at all because it's going to the wrong address,' says Michael Critelli, CEO of Pitney Bowes, the Fortune 500 maker of mailing equipment and software."

We have the ability to communicate more clearly, to streamline our number of choices, to tighten the gap between promotion and practice, to more widely and effectively integrate the "human touch" in our organization, and to—as Pitney Bowes' Critelli implies—get it right at Level One. That's easier said than done. But in the real world, you simply must execute the approaches listed here to move your customers and prospects (and, perhaps, even your employees) from the fog of confusion into the sunlight of connection.

Executive Summary

The Fifth Disconnection is that what customers REALLY want is coordination —however, most organizations offer them confusion.

- When the customer perceives a lack of coordination, confusion usually results, creating a disconnection between the organization and the customer. It seems as though everyone has a story to describe a personal experience where confusion was somehow created by an organization—whether it is someplace we work, purchase from for our respective employers, or do personal shopping.

- Sometimes people in our organization seek to place the blame for the confusion on the customer. And, let's face it, sometimes customers do and say some pretty silly things. However, there's no reason a customer should know our business as well as we do. Our job is to eliminate confusion at all levels of interaction and reconnect with those customers.
- No matter what the customer says and does, they may not always be right—but he or she is always the customer!

- Sometimes confusion in the marketplace is intentionally generated by our competitors.
  - You cannot help it if another organization has the unethical approach of trying to make themselves look better by misrepresenting your products and services.
  - There are examples in politics that clearly display that deception is worse than mere derogatory comments.
  - Respond to this type of intentional confusion and misrepresentation with emotion first, then evidence. The unethical approach of a competitor is geared to create an emotional response from the customer or prospect. Therefore, you must respond first with emotion to counter it.

- Many times, however, we inadvertently create confusion among our own customers and prospects through the five major causes of customer confusion:
  - *Overwhelming number of choices*
    - We offer so many products and options that most customers simply can't keep up—so they go elsewhere.
  - *Incongruence between promotion and practice*
    - Through our marketing, we create in the customer's mind an expectation of an experience that we cannot, or do not, deliver.

- *Technology vs. human touch*
  - Efforts to streamline and expand the technological efficiencies possible create confusion among customers seeking a "real person" to give them answers.
- *Inability to execute at Level One creates disconnection at higher levels*
  - Why should customers feel we can deliver on Levels Two and Three when we can't get their bills correct or execute simple processing in an efficient manner?
- *Technical communication presented to a nontechnical audience*
  - Often technical communication is marred by the efforts of the presenters to overwhelm the intended audience with information.
  - The "Logos, Ethos, Pathos" approach of Aristotle is still relevant and should be applied in technical communication.
    - *Logos*—an appeal through the argument of the apparent truth of the matter being presented; most often the course taken by technical professionals as they communicate.
    - *Ethos*—an appeal based upon the character and credibility of the presenter; an approach that is well received by many who expect the opinions and recommendations of a skilled professional to be of value.
    - *Pathos*—an appeal to the emotions of the audience; most often overlooked in business. To be compelling, we must connect with the emotions of employees, customers, and prospects.

Bridge Building
Moving from Confusion to Coordination

- Do you believe the right hand knows what the left is doing within your organization?

- Name two instances where company policy makes it difficult for customers to do business with you.

- Is it possible that your customers are confused? How? (Remember, it could be their fault they are confused, yet you still have to take the initiative to set it right.)

- Does your sales and marketing play more into facts or emotions? How about your competitor's? Has your competitor created confusion about your organization and your products and services in the marketplace? How are you responding?

- How many choices and options do you make available to your customers? Have you considered that you may be confusing them with a plethora of options?

- Show three ways in which your marketing is congruent with the actual practice of your organization. Are there any specific areas where you feel the customer may perceive that you are stretching the truth a bit?

- Call your company and order something. Call your customer service line and report a problem. How do you critically evaluate the blend of technology versus the human element that customers really want?

- Pretend for a moment that you are a football coach. (I tend to shy away from using the clichéd athletic analogies, however, this one fits the bill.) Envision the execution of Level One activities as an offensive line that must block and tackle for the rest of the team. How would you rate their performance? Are they assisting or hindering your ability to score touchdowns?

○ Don't forget—you're the coach! How will you coach your team in a way that inspires them to improve their performance?

- Will you teach fundamentals?
- Will you draw up new plays?
- Will you go out and get better linemen?

- Take one specific product or service of your organization. Develop three short presentations (let's say, for example, two minutes in length) with each utilizing a different form of Aristotle's forms of persuasion: Ethos, Pathos, Logos. Share your presentations with a friend who does not thoroughly know your product. Ask your friend to evaluate the level of persuasion from each presentation. Then, blend the high points from each presentation to create just one.

6

THE SIXTH DISCONNECTION

What Customers REALLY Want: *Innovation*
What Business Offers: *Status Quo*

We've established that many of our customers are bored by the same choices, same products, same services, same old, same old.

So, what does most business offer? Status quo.

Many companies seem to be saying, "You liked it last year; you'll like it this year . . . next year too. Sure, we'll make some little incremental improvements and tinker with things just a bit. But, hey, why be innovative when we have something that already works? Didn't you ever hear of 'New Coke'?"

In an editorial in the trade journal *Modern Materials Handling*, Raymond A. Kulwiec wrote, "Regarded as an important tool, continuous improvement is being practiced not only by companies that seek world-class status, but also by those that want ISO 9000 certification, or win a Baldridge quality award. The problem is that *continuous improvement inhibits innovation*. If a company were to choose between innovation and continuous improvement, the choice *must* be innovation."

Customers want you to "wow" them. They want to believe that what keeps you awake at night is contemplating how to revolutionize your service or product in a manner that knocks it out of the park for them. They crave innovation. They're getting the status quo.

Do you honestly believe that the fervent desire of any customer is that you improve your process management by 0.03 percent? If you want to create what customers REALLY want, . . . *create!* Become passionate about innovation!

You can develop originality within a product or service that you—or someone else—are already providing. Richard Branson, the flamboyant chairman and CEO of Virgin Group, has innovated in every industry he has touched—from selling music to transcontinental travel. There are innovators in small businesses in just about every small community. How do we know? They survived the Wal-Mart onslaught in their towns. Whether it was the local grocery store that continues to exist because of innovating custom-cut meats and home delivery (like my father did in our hometown), or a sporting goods store that led with the novelty of let-

If you want to create what customers REALLY want, . . . *create!* Become passionate about innovation!

ting you try out the equipment and get a feel for what you're buying, innovation is found in many places. Unfortunately, many of us fail to get saved by the "religion of innovation" until it's too late.

As mentioned earlier, the classic opening line of *Good to Great* is: "Good is the enemy of great." When we devote all our efforts to continual incremental improvements, maintaining the status quo, and disregarding innovation, we are merely accepting the good—and we are choosing to not take a shot at becoming great.

Incremental Improvement as a Corporate Way of Life

We were all caught up in it.

Several years ago, when it seemed as though the Japanese knew everything about business—and the press was making it out to appear that American companies understood very little—the hot word was *kaizen*. The word is a Japanese term that means "continuous improvement," based on the words *kai*, roughly translated "constant," and *zen*, which means something like "enhancement." Motivational speaker Tony Robbins even created his own version called CANI—an acronym for "Constant And Never-ending Improvement." Organizations from one end of the country to the other sponsored "kaizen seminars" to determine how they could set about the task of constant improvement of their products, services, and processes.

We're *still* caught up in it.

It has a more precise formula now and a different name. Yet "continuous improvement" is still the goal, even when you call it Six Sigma. The Web site www.iSixSigma.com defines the Six Sigma process as "a rigorous and a systematic methodology that utilizes information (management by facts) and statistical analysis to measure and improve a company's operational performance, practices and systems by identifying and preventing 'defects' in manufacturing and service-related processes in order to anticipate and exceed expectations of all stakeholders to accomplish effectiveness."

Another interesting position of the Six Sigma approach is that by making decisions based on precise information created by your measurements, you can enhance your customer focus. ("Reducing variation in your business allows you to make customer-focused, data-driven decisions," according to Six Sigma experts.)

I imagine you already know that there are various "warfare" metaphors in Six Sigma that are applied in order to create the analogy of fighting defects in the manufacturing process and winning the battle for perfection. Those who have advanced in their understanding and training in the principles of Six Sigma earn, literally, a designation called the "Black Belt."

In an article titled "Innovation and Imitation—Positional Determinants of Success and Failure," the Wharton School states, "Business in today's dynamic economy *requires* that firms constantly improve existing products *or* offer new ones in order to stay competitive."[1] In other words, you have to keep making your products and services really, genuinely better—not just trifle with a few details. Or you have to create new approaches to your service and new creative features in your products—or new products altogether—to keep your organizational head above water in our twenty-first-century world.

Yet there are hundreds of companies out there that initiated Six Sigma programs for one very important reason (to them): *The competition was doing it.*

The modern organization's challenge, though, is obvious—innovation is expensive, difficult, potentially unrewarding, and more than a little scary. Many companies that have used creativity to introduce new products look forward to the time when they can merely focus on improvements rather than innovation. For Microsoft to create PowerPoint was originality at its finest. This year's upgrade doesn't have to be. Guess which is easier and less expensive? A company can never forget that without constant innovation, there isn't a compelling product there to be improved.

Innovation Means Enhanced Business

The facts supporting the premise that there are positive consequences of rapid product innovation—and that it plays a role in creating organizational success—are convincing. This theory was proved by Joseph T. Vesey in his research for the article "The New Competitors: They think in terms of speed to market," for the Academy of Management Executives. As reported by Behna N. Tabrizi in *Administrative Science Quarterly*, this study of innovative product introductions illustrated that products that were "six months late in entering the market, but were within budget, earned *33 percent less* over a five-year period than they would have if on time. Entering the market on time—*even 50 percent over budget*—reduced a firm's profitability by *only 4 percent* for that product (emphasis added)"[2]

It also seems that it is just common sense to assume the companies that have declared war on inefficiency in their organization are also the ones most likely to have difficulty with the creative process. It's a messy thing. Give me a billion dollars and five years and I still cannot promise you that I'll come up with the next big thing. Yet two young guys in a garage with practically no money can create the personal computer. Six Sigma *that*.

Ron Jonash, vice president and director of technology and innovation at management consulting firm Arthur D. Little, wrote in *USA Today Sunday* magazine that "consistent breakthrough product innovation rewards all of an organization's shareholders."[3] (However, as a board member of a public company, I'd suggest it also means they will have to wait a little longer than just a single quarterly earnings report.)

Jonash suggests there are additional benefits to innovation, as well. "Customers, employees, and business partners benefit, too. Customers are more excited and more satisfied," he stated.

> Give me a billion dollars and five years and I still cannot promise you that I'll come up with the next big thing. Yet two young guys in a garage with practically no money can create the personal computer. Six Sigma *that*.

The innovator's improved performance and value leadership strengthen customer relationships and open new ones. Market share and brand equity grow as customer loyalty builds. Employees are more loyal, so they stay on the job. Moreover, employees at innovative companies are more highly motivated; they may participate in the ownership of the company; and they presumably will share in its rising fortunes in the form of salary increases—all of which makes retaining them easier.[4]

Consider once again the CCA—Continuous Compelling Advantage—and its significance here. Certainly the term *Continuous* implies that what is involved is no "one-shot" type of approach. To strengthen your Compelling Advantage, you must be continually working to improve it, to make it more persuasive. Harley-Davidson provides a great example. In an article in *American Machinist*, it was described in this manner:

> Harley's quest to streamline operations is based on a philosophy of continuous improvement. Since the buyback, the firm resisted resting on its past achievements or reputation. This determination to stay ahead of the curve seems to be as alive and well today as it was in 1985. As (Tom) Gelb (former vice president of manufacturing) described the firm's dedication to process improvement in 1985: "It's not a program, it's a journey to efficiency that goes on forever."

No one would dispute that it makes great sense for Harley to seek alternative methods on a consistent basis to improve processes—and motorcycles—every single day. On the other hand, no one would argue with the assertion that Harley already has a Continuous Compelling Advantage in the motorcycle industry. The innovation in the sound, look, and feel of a Harley provides a CCA that makes its competitors' imitations irrelevant. If any other manufacturer of motorcycles wants to compete with Harley-Davidson, wouldn't it be better off trying to create a new innovation to inspire both its customer base and prospective buyers than to imitate the Harley? Do you think any imitator has a chance to "out-Harley" the real thing?

Keep the Perspective

The point here is that customers are uninfluenced by minor incremental improvements or apparent imitations. It's not that it is unimportant to improve what your organization sells—it *obviously* is! However, when you combine the challenges we've spoken of earlier—customer boredom, lack of emotional connections, reduction in client loyalty, and many more—it becomes easier to see why better taillights on this year's model, or answering the phone on the third instead of the fourth ring, fails to create a powerful Continuous Compelling Advantage. The CCA is where your focus should be. Constant improvement of a mediocre and noncompelling product or service is like the old cliché about rearranging the deck chairs on the *Titanic*. Be bold! Show customers that you deserve their loyalty, because you're willing to innovate for their benefit.

Let me also propose to you that while it's easy to be completely supportive of the Six Sigma and kaizen efforts that have made a remarkable impact on productivity, process upgrading, and driving down the number of defects, I also believe that (like anything else in business or life) too much of a good thing can create less-than-desirable results. If you're making only incremental improvements (as difficult as that may be) and benchmarking yourself against your competitors in your industry, you may be painting your organization—and your customers—into a box where neither of you wants to be.

Customers do not need another imitation of what's already available. As the saying goes, "Been there. Done that." We want innovation! We want compelling products and services that amaze and inspire us. You say that sounds nice, but you're in a commodity business? Well, remember the earlier examples of Starbucks in the commodity business of coffee and Evian in the commodity business of water? Commodity is no excuse—there's still a way to be innovative. As Ron Jonash advocated in his article about innovation:

> Commoditization drags down all of a company's products or services. Companies that face commoditization of one or more of their products or services can't grow. Profit margins shrink. Shareholder expectations for growth oblige management to create long-term value at an unprecedented rate. However, a firm's usual product pipeline, traditional mergers and acquisitions strategy, level of continuous operations improvement, and ongoing market expansion efforts usually aren't sufficient to meet rising earnings expectations in today's markets.

Not a pretty picture, is it?

Please don't misinterpret the point—you *must* always strive to improve what you're currently doing. It's just that incremental improvements do not inspire customer loyalty. To provide what customers REALLY want, you must foster the improvement process— *and* be wildly passionate about innovation!

Dangers of Being an Imitator, Rather Than an Innovator

Previously, we've discussed the pitfalls of commoditization and the power of differentiation. We have advanced the idea of the CCA (Continuous Compelling Advantage) as a way to begin evaluating your ability to provide what customers REALLY want. As we discuss the final major customer disconnection, we will discover that innovation is the approach that can provide you with both the differentiation that will create the unique place in the customers' "mindshare" that you desire, and the CCA that will engender their lasting loyalty.

Some organizations merely imitate their competition. They have somehow developed the twisted logic that if customers like the originator, they'll like the imitator, as well. They don't set trends; they follow them. The R & D department—if existent—is to figure out how to duplicate rather than create. They'll take the idea of another and try to find a way to do it cheaper and faster—but not necessarily *better*—than their competition.

Let's examine the dangers of imitation as another way to propose that innovation is the strategy to overcome customer disconnections. Here are just four of the pitfalls encountered by imitating organizations:

1. You can only be as good as what you imitate.

2. You fail to create customer loyalty.

3. You're at the mercy of the competition's innovations.

4. You don't inspire your employees with a vision of imitation.

You Can Only Be as Good as What You Imitate

First, let's be very clear—by "imitation" I don't mean an activity as extreme as crafting a knockoff Louis Vuitton purse. I don't even suggest it's akin to downloading music and burning CDs to sell. That's copying . . . *and* that's illegal.

The meaning of *imitation* for our discussion here is "something made to be as much as possible like something else." And, like most innovators, I don't believe imitation is the "sincerest form of flattery."

It's a competitive maneuver—and one that provides few long-term rewards for any organization.

A very dramatic argument against imitation was found in an article from the January 1997 issue of the *Harvard Business Review* titled "Value Innovation: The Strategic Logic of High Growth," by W. Chan Kim and Renee Mauborgne. They wrote:

> In a five-year study of high-growth companies and their less successful competitors, we found that the answer lies in the way each group approached strategy. The difference in approach was not a matter of managers choosing one analytical tool or planning model over another. The difference was in the companies' fundamental, implicit assumptions about strategy. The less successful companies took a conventional approach: their strategic thinking was dominated by the idea of staying ahead of the competition. In stark contrast, the high-growth companies paid little attention to matching or beating their rivals. Instead, they sought to *make their competitors irrelevant* through a strategic logic we call value innovation. (Emphasis added)

In other words, the less successful companies took the approach of imitation—and their very act of imitating unintentionally added to the relevancy and success of the company and products they were mimicking. The more highly successful companies cared less about their competitors. They put their resources and efforts into innovation instead of incremental improvements or imitation.

When I first started in the field of professional speaking, my mentor and hero was a humorist named Grady Nutt. Grady had been a minister at a small church in Kentucky. He began entertaining youth groups with humorous stories about experiences from his early life in Texas, especially his growing up in a small Southern Baptist church. He had gained a national reputation as a speaker because of the insight his stories provided and the laughter his monologues provoked. He had appeared numerous times on the *Mike Douglas Show* in its heyday and had become a regular on the classic country comedy show *Hee Haw*. Grady was a great dichotomy—he gained fame through his stories of small-town preachers and church-related bloopers, yet he was one of the most profound thinkers and discerning men I've ever known. Grady's way of writing and telling a story had a deep impact on me—so much so that I tried to sound like him—in fact, I wanted to *be* him!

One day Grady called me and asked to take me out to lunch—an honor I quickly accepted. In his kind and gentle manner over the table he told me he was flattered that I appreciated his talent so much. Then, he dropped the bomb that was the reason for lunch—and a pivotal moment in my life. "Scott," he said, "there's something else you must consider. As long as you keep trying to be the next Grady Nutt, then second place is the best you can possibly hope for. My advice to you is to seek to become the best Scott McKain you can possibly be."

> Whether it's in show business or your business, the imitators are never as good as the original—and they become defined by the original.

I sat there stunned, and a little embarrassed. Yet I also had what I like to call the "blinding flash of the obvious." With the exception of celebrities like Rich Little, no one has ever imitated his or her way to success and greatness. (And, in fact, the impersonator—by definition—will never be as famous as those he parodies.)

Whether it's in show business or your business, the imitators are never as good as the original—and they become defined by the original.

I realized I needed to follow a different route than my mentor or I would always find myself in the same classification as he. I had a natural interest in the way business works—my parents were entrepreneurs with a small-town grocery store—so I changed direction and pursued a different career. Now, thirty years later, I can look back and be happy about that decision.

You can only be as good as what you imitate. If you decide to follow the strategy of replication or simulation, the absolute best you can hope for is to come in second.

You Fail to Create Customer Loyalty

In his terrific book *Becoming a Category of One* (Wiley, 2003), my good friend Joe Calloway describes several innovative steps that organizations made to expand their growth and profitability. One of the benefits they discovered from their innovations is that their customers became those "raving fans" we're all seeking.

When United Airlines created its "airline-within-an-airline"—Ted—it jumped on the imitation bandwagon. United watched as jetBlue and Southwest grew in passengers and profitability, and naturally it wanted some of that for its company. The trouble was, by adopting the "me too" approach, it reduced the loyalty of the customers it was already serving. While most of us flying United were on that carrier precisely because we did not want the "discount airline" experience, United gave additional legitimacy to that approach via its imitation strategy. In other words, United failed on the maxim stated earlier—it achieved "legitimacy by being similar to them"—but it has not "simultaneously secured competitiveness by being different from their competitors." The result is that its best customers aren't being inspired to remain loyal. Many of them—like me—are inspired to take our business elsewhere.

Instead, Continental Airlines is taking a different and innovative approach. According to *Business Week* magazine, the airline

has started rolling out a Customer Information System where every one of its 43,000 gate, reservation, and service agents will immediately know the history and value of each customer. A so-called intelligent engine not only mines data on status but also suggests remedies and perks, from automatic coupons for service delays to priority for upgrades, giving the carrier more consistency in staff behavior and service delivery. The technology will even allow Continental staff to note details about the preferences of top customers so the airline can offer them extra services. As [Vice President of marketing, sales and distribution, Bonnie Reitz] puts it: "We even know if they put their eyeshades on and go to sleep." Such tiering pays off. Thanks to its heavy emphasis on top-tier clients, about 47% of Continental's customers now pay higher-cost, unrestricted fares, up from 38% in 1995.[5]

Continental—through the use of technology to deliver innovative and improved service—is creating higher revenue through enhanced customer loyalty.

In sports, like it or not, there are millions of "fair-weather fans." If you don't believe that, then just look and see how many people around the country are currently wearing jerseys from the Chicago Bulls. When Michael Jordan was in his prime, you would see the Bulls #23 everywhere in the country. Now that the Bulls are having a tough time, they've not only lost games, but they've lost an exponentially greater amount of merchandise sales.

The point is, no one is clamoring to root for a team thoroughly devoted to *not* leading the division. (The victory by the Boston Red Sox in the 2004 World Series proved their fans didn't want them to be "lovable losers"—instead they cheered them on to a World Championship!!) Likewise, boring imitation does not inspire customers to become *your* raving fans . . . and your customers want to do business not with "lovable losers"—but instead the champions of providing what they *really* want. They want you to be to your field what the Red Sox became in theirs.

You're at the Mercy of the Competition's Innovations

Obviously. If you weren't, you would not be an imitator.

Imitators are always playing catch-up with their innovative competition. They always have to be on guard for the next new thing so they can find some way to replicate it.

Take razors, for example. For many years, Schick was perceived to be the imitator, while Gillette was the innovator. Schick was a distant number two, seemingly content to attempt to replicate Gillette's advances and sell a lot of cheap, disposable razors. "It's somewhat of a classic situation of a market that was stable, where people had agreed on their roles," said William R. Bishop Jr., a consumer retail consultant in Chicago to the *Washington Post*. "Now," he added, "Schick is out to change that. So this is something the people at Gillette have to take seriously."

When Energizer Holdings, Inc.—a company better known for batteries (and innovation)—purchased Schick, things began to change. As reported by the *Washington Post* in January 2004:

> In September, it [Schick] introduced Quattro, the world's first four-blade razor, claiming it gives men the deepest, nick-less shave. Schick's sleek, hyper-modern razor is a direct challenge to Gillette's premium Mach3 line, which since its introduction six years ago has boasted in television and print ads that its three-blade razors, tipped with irritation-minimizing aloe and vitamin E, offer "the world's closest shave." Energizer reported sales of $703.5 million, *a 59 percent increase* from the same period last year.[6]

Ask Schick about imitation versus innovation. When they "knew their role," they watched as their competitor won more than 70 percent of the market share. Now, no longer content to watch and wait for Gillette's next innovation, it is a hotter brand than it has been in ages—perhaps ever.

You Don't Inspire Your Employees with a Vision of Imitation

At Pyramid Coach, we like to believe we have been innovative in our industry—luxury coach travel for entertainers. Well, maybe I shouldn't restrict it to entertainers, because one of our innovations was the use of our buses for new applications, like taking several friends on a golf trip. Any number of guys, for example, can lease a bus for a week and travel from course to course while enjoying the trip, sleeping in the bunks, and bragging when they get back home that they toured in Brad Paisley, Chicago, or Britany Spears' bus!

This approach benefits us in a big way, as well. The time most groups want to go on a golf trip is in the winter—our typical customer group consists of eight guys from the Midwest. This is precisely the time our coaches are underutilized, because there are significantly fewer concerts in the winter than in the summer months.

One of the significant benefits we've received is that our drivers are very motivated—they get to do things they've never done before, as well as work in what is usually considered a very slow season. And a company that innovates is a company perceived to be more exciting than its competitors. Would you rather work for a progressive company—or one that shoots for the middle? Your colleagues feel the same way!

People become inspired by vision and great ideas. Change the thinking for a moment and consider a political election. Those office seekers who inspire the electorate aren't the ones talking about incremental improvement and imitation of the programs and systems found in other countries. The ones who have innovative ideas, and passionately express those concepts, are the ones who change the nation. If it sways votes, why wouldn't it move employees?

Why Innovation?

Do customers really want innovation? Maybe not. They probably won't express it in that manner. By definition, an innovation is something that isn't currently in the marketplace, so in most cases your customer hasn't even thought of it yet. None of us were sitting around wondering where we could buy a little gadget that played cassette tapes so we could walk around with headphones and listen. Yet the Sony Walkman was an innovation that we gobbled up by the millions.

And, as a side note, isn't it interesting that in many situations, innovative companies become happy after an innovation and stop pushing for more new and great stuff? There's no reason that the company that gave us the Walkman failed to give us the iPod. There's no excuse for the corporation that had the good sense to create *Sports Illustrated* to not also come up with ESPN. Why couldn't Maxwell House or Folger's—with such an amazing head start—have developed what we now know as Starbucks?

As the headline of a *Fortune* magazine article from October 2, 2000, written by Nicholas Stein says: "The World's Most Admired Companies:

How Do You Make the List? Innovate, Innovate, Innovate." However, don't just consider the current state of your organization—think about the future. Ask yourself this question: How are my products and services different today than they were a year ago? Five years ago? Ten years ago? If your answer is "not very," then how are you keeping pace with the generational changes that are happening? You're not.

"Companies that ignore the tastes of today's 21-year-olds do so at their peril. If a brand missed the 21-year-olds of Gen X, it could survive because that audience was relatively small. Not so with Gen Y. These newly minted adults are the bellwether of what the nation's consumers will soon be doing, buying and thinking," writes Michael J. Weiss in *American Demographics*. He continues:

> Born in 1982, today's 21-year-olds are barely old enough to remember when Ronald Reagan was president. Yet in their lifetimes, American society has changed dramatically. Immigration has made the country much more diverse: 1 in 3 21-year-olds are not Caucasian. Family structures have also changed: 1 in 4 21-year-olds were raised by a single parent; 3 in 4 have working mothers. And while their parents are still prone to view the Internet and mobile phones as novelties, 21-year-olds have literally grown up with them and incorporated them into every aspect of their lives. According to the Bureau of Labor Statistics, some 70 percent of them already hold a full- or part-time job.[7]

My nephew, Benjamin, perfectly fits this category. He is a twenty-three-year-old who was raised by a single working mother. You'll usually find him either on the Internet or on his mobile phone. He's working a full-time job, yet certainly doesn't expect to retire there. He just purchased a new Toyota Scion. Why? It has an ear-splitting sound system that plays MP3 music files from his computer. It has a 15-volt outlet so he can plug his laptop into his car. It looks like a box on wheels. I find it ugly beyond belief. He sees it as cool beyond description.

It's interesting to me that he never says he has a "Toyota." He will tell you he drives a "Scion." It's not the brand that is important. It's the *car* that is the innovation, in his way of thinking. He's emotionally linked with the innovations of the car—not the manufacturer (which, of course, raises very interesting questions about his future loyalty as a customer).

The Scion is a particularly good example of the importance of innovation. Incrementally improving the Celica—a car that I was excited to own in 1982, when my nephew was born—would have done nothing to appeal to a customer like Benjamin. *Innovation* made all the difference in getting this sale for Toyota. If you wonder about the passion customers have for innovation, consider that my nephew tracked down his Scion on the Internet, because there was a waiting period of a few months to get one at the several local dealers he shopped. Since *none* of them created a relationship with him—and, therefore, didn't offer to be his partner in purchasing a Scion—he traveled from Indiana to *West Virginia* to make his proud purchase! And, by the way, he paid full sticker price.

Why innovate? There are literally thousands of reasons. Here is perhaps the best one: if you don't keep innovating, Benjamin and the millions like him won't buy anything from you.

Look Around You

Take a look around your office and see how much diversity you have. Certainly, it is a priority to have gender and ethnic diversity within an office. However, I believe we too many times stop at that point.

> If two people think exactly alike, one is unnecessary.

How are you doing in terms of age diversity? I hate it that my new cell phone will not let me increase the size of the font on the screen. I'm sure the thirty-five-year-old who designed it likes it just fine—her eyes are probably a lot better than those of a guy about to turn fifty. But at some point in the process, why didn't they ask a person in the fifty-to-sixty-five age-group if he could read the numbers? My guess is there weren't any people around them they could ask.

Do you think for a moment that a group of fifty-five-year-old men and women came up with the Scion because they knew what Generation Y wanted in a car? Of course not. You make that group a part of the process, beginning with the concept, even before product design.

How about diversity of thought? Is it rampant where you work? It should be. It's been said many times, but if two people think exactly alike, one is unnecessary. If you've surrounded yourself with other professionals who think just like you, you're missing many great ideas. *And you're missing the intellectual growth that occurs when our minds are challenged by alternative ways of thinking.*

I've discovered this principle on a very personal level. When I was growing up, I was surrounded by the other good people of the Methodist church of my hometown. A great part of my spiritual life was simply doing what everyone else was doing. I thought my faith was strong, but I was wrong.

Until my beliefs were challenged—first at college and later in life by a friend who is an atheist—I hadn't developed the intellectual depth in my spiritual convictions to be able to withstand a confrontation against my faith, much less be persuasive in a theological argument. I realized that being involved with people who thought differently was, in fact, something that strengthened my personal faith because of the intellectual rigor required to stand up for my beliefs.

One of the great gifts you can give yourself is to hire someone who thinks and acts differently from you. Hire a twenty-one-year-old, Generation-Y young woman who dresses in clothes you can't stand. What about a seventy-year-young senior citizen who still wants to contribute and who honestly believes he may be around for another three decades?

Many managers never get divergent styles of people around them, perhaps because somewhere in their hearts they realize their convictions about business may not be able to stand the rigors of a variety of intellectual input. Just as in my story about my personal faith, these folks really need to be challenged to become stronger.

Diversity of Thought Breeds Innovation

I was speaking to a group of real estate agents a few years ago. During the question-and-answer session following my presentation, a young woman stood up and said, "I'm just beginning my career in real estate. Could you tell me, if you were showing a house to a couple, what you would say?"

After thinking for a moment, it occurred to me. "First off," I responded, "I would—if at all possible—be meeting with them in their current residence. I would ask them to take me on a tour of their current home. I would attempt to get the couple to describe in detail to me what they are going to miss the most about their home when they move into the new house they are about to buy. Then, when I took them on showings, I would describe aspects in the home in relation to what they loved about the current house. And, of course, I would also be able to tell them how the house I was showing them would help them overcome the points of their current home they wanted to improve."

A senior real estate agent raised her hand and said, "Did you just think of that?" I replied that the answer was yes—it was the first time I had ever considered the question.

"I've been in the business for several years," she said, "and that's the first time I've heard that idea. It's great." The audience then started to applaud. Someone else made a very generous remark about my supposed intellect, and I had to set him straight. I was not able to come up with that idea because I'm particularly smart; it's because *I'm not a real estate agent!* Remember the old saying "You can't see the forest for the trees"? The same principle was at work here!

> Fresh eyes come up with fresh ideas.

Part of the reason most organizations focus on incremental improvement is that it's the same old team always working on the service or product. If you've been looking at something for years, it's hard to all of a sudden think of some new, innovative idea regarding its design or use. Ask yourself how you can involve someone from another department. How about someone you know who is really smart and has never used the product or needed the service? How about a customer? How about a *former* customer? Fresh eyes come up with fresh ideas.

Here's the Bottom Line on Innovation

At the end of the day, not only do your customers really want you to be innovative; it is necessary for your organization, no matter what you do. In *Fast Company* magazine, Gary Hamel, author of *Leading the Revolution: How to Thrive in Turbulent Times by Making Innovation a Way of Life*, wrote:

> Most companies today can't grow revenue by flogging the same old stuff to the same old customers through the same old channels in the same old way. People may already be eating as many hamburgers as they are ever going to eat, drinking as much beer as they are ever going to drink, even buying as many plain vanilla personal computers as they are ever going to buy. But customers will always make room for something new, useful, and value packed. Consider DoCoMo, the Japanese company that developed an Internet-enabled mobile phone. Its I-mode service attracted 30 million customers in 30 months. Sure, you can grow today. But only if you bring something unexpected and exciting to your customers.[8]

Yet now more than ever before, we hear managers encouraging their colleagues to—ready for the trite phrase?—"think outside the box." If that's the case, why is there so little in the way of innovation?

The answer is fairly simple: managers fail to encourage their people to "*do* outside the box"! While creative, innovative thinking may be encouraged, working and managing that way are not. We're taught in school to "color inside the lines"—and at work, most of us have been encouraged to follow a similar philosophy.

Also, many times employees are sent mixed messages, and they convey that inconsistency to your customers. They're encouraged to "do whatever it takes" to keep the customers happy—yet are also beaten on to keep costs as low as possible. They have heard how they need to "create relationships with customers"—from the same managers who refuse to listen to innovative ideas and decline to execute creative practices. If your employee is uncertain of the message you are sending her, how can you expect her to take innovative approaches to customer retention?

In addition, innovation must have a means of transference within the organization. By that I mean you must not only conceive of a creative idea and plan its execution; you must also focus on how that innovation and its practice will be transferred throughout your business. Do you have educational sessions? Do you create a video on it? Do you provide a manual for all employees? No matter what action you take, you must take action. For your employees to be the means of transference to your customers, you have to consider an "internal advertising campaign" to sell the innovation internally prior to external exposure.

> The bottom line is that innovation is good for the bottom line.

As many innovation experts suggest, one of the management challenges is that a manager may assume if there are a hundred different creative ideas, his or her staff could be going in a hundred different directions. The manager's challenge is to encourage and reward customer-focused innovation and develop models and methods to create the sharper vision to bring the best ideas to the forefront.

Heinz's president and CEO for European operations, Joe Jimenez, said, "The strategy is [for] top line growth through innovation. Bottom line growth will follow." According to *Grocer* magazine, "Heinz has redefined its new product development process as it seeks to re-energize its European business and drive category growth."[9]

Jimenez created an "Innovations Executive Committee" from across Europe consisting of twelve top marketing and technical directors. "Previously everyone got a little resource and we were not fully supporting new innovations," Jiminez commented. "There was not a lot of analytical rigor. The innovations team is designed to fix this. We will put the resource into backing new, bigger ideas and invest more in analysis."

But the bottom line is that innovation is good for the bottom line. It enhances customer excitement and loyalty toward your organization. It helps to inspire employees to deliver at a higher level, and builds their organizational loyalty, as well. It generates recognition within your industry and community as it provides a differentiating factor from that horde of businesses that, through their actions or inaction, merely advance the status quo of which the customer is so tired.

As *Information Week* reported on a presentation they sponsored of legendary GE CEO Jack Welch, "He said that while he always valued inventions and big ideas, he put a far greater value on people who could take those ideas and spread them, share them, move them through the company in ways that would make the customer happier and more engaged."[10]

Who are we to argue with one of the most respected and successful managers, innovators, and leaders in the history of corporate America?

Executive Summary

The Sixth Disconnection is that what customers REALLY want is innovation—however, most organizations maintain the status quo.

- The continuous improvement that most organizations strive for may actually be inhibiting innovation.
  - By choosing to devote major resources to simply enhance the status quo, organizations are choosing the "good" rather than the "great."
  - There are many detailed corporate strategies for incremental improvement but fewer strategies for innovation.
  - Innovation is a risky business. However, by not pursuing a course of creativity, you may be dooming yourself.
- Create a "Continuous Compelling Advantage" (CCA).
  - Innovation means enhanced business. Being first to market—even if you're over budget—can mean greatly enhanced earnings.

- ○ CCA is an ongoing effort to provide customers with innovative, compelling reasons to do business with you.
- ○ The constant improvement of non-compelling products, features, and services is futile.

- Every leader should understand that there are inherent—and often overlooked—dangers in pursuing the course of imitation:
  - ○ *You're only as good as what you imitate.*
  - ○ *You fail to enhance customer loyalty.*
  - ○ *You're at the mercy of the competition's innovations.*
  - ○ *You don't inspire employees with a vision of imitation.*

- Why innovation?
  - ○ By definition, an *innovation* is something that isn't already in the market. That makes it a tough choice on the part of managers. Your customers probably aren't clamoring for it.
  - ○ You need innovation because there is a new generation of customers coming. Generation Y has dramatically different views and wants. Without innovation your organization will become demographically irrelevant.
  - ○ Diversity inspires innovation. Without diversity of thought, you're missing great ideas and intellectual growth.

- The bottom line on innovation
  - "You can only grow by bringing something unexpected and exciting to customers" (Gary Hamel). Unfortunately, the same managers who encourage colleagues to think outside the box often restrict their ability to *do* outside the box.
  - Don't forget that your employees are your means of transference of innovation to your customers. Sell the innovations internally, prior to external exposure.

- As former General Electric CEO Jack Welch said, "Innovation is of great value—but there is a far greater value on the *people* who share and execute those ideas in ways that engage the customer."

Bridge Building
Moving from Status Quo to Innovation

- On a scale of 1 to 10, how would you rate your passion for innovation?
  - Ask five colleagues to evaluate themselves as well on this question.
  - Then, have each of the five score the rest of the group on the same question.
  - Get together with your group of five and discuss any gaps between the perceptions that an individual has regarding her passion for innovation and the score the rest of the group gave her. Why do those disconnections exist?
- This chapter mentioned several business visionaries who are true innovators. Who do you admire for his or her ability to think creatively? List three and then add a short statement about the innovation or inspired solution that captured your imagination.
- How has incremental improvement stifled innovation within your organization?
- Let's repeat a question: What is your Continuous Compelling Advantage? How are you using innovation to continue to be compelling? How are you improving process management to continue to have an advantage?
- What company policies or initiatives in your organization could be perceived by your employees as overkill. In other words, where are you guilty of overdoing a good thing?

- Do your organization's products or services imitate a competitor's in any area? Does that approach limit your innovation to only be as good (or bad) as they are?

- Cite four points of innovation in your products or services and how these aspects drive customer loyalty. (If you can't do it, your customers can't either.)

- Do your employees believe that your organization is innovative? Do they perceive the opportunity to make great things and do cool stuff? Is there, perhaps, any correlation to your answer here and the rate of employee turnover in your organization (particularly with workers under 35)?

- Would your organization receive high marks if your employees were polled on the "Most Admired Companies" or "Best Companies to Work For" lists?

- How significant is the diversity of thought and behavior in your organization? Do you need to take steps to enhance this type of diversity?

- Finally—and please be brutally honest here—is there a chance that you are selling the same old stuff in the same old way to the same old customers?

  ○ If so, do you realize what is so awfully wrong with that approach? Do you understand how dangerous that is?

7

CONCLUSION: THE CULTURE OF THE CUSTOMER

An old joke back home in my small town in Indiana is that the only culture we have there is *agri*culture. I now live in that cultural mecca called "Las Vegas," where, until recently, the most attended museum in the community celebrated the life of Liberace.

What is a "culture," anyway? The *Encarta World English Dictionary* describes it as "the beliefs, customs, practices, and social behavior of a particular nation or people." So, what are the beliefs, customs, practices, and behavior of your organization's people? How does the customer perceive it? Have you made a concerted effort to create a central culture for your organization—or to evaluate, revise, and improve the one you already have?

You'd better. Because the next definition in the dictionary is: "a group of people whose shared beliefs and practices identify the particular place, class, or time to which they belong." In an organizational sense, that means customers use the shared practices of how your people behave to serve as a method to identify them. If you don't believe that, ask a Saturn automobile customer how the people at that dealership behave compared to employees at other places where they have purchased cars. Customers believe that Saturn must have a different culture—because the shared practices displayed by its people identify it to customers as unique and compelling.

Rethink and Reinvent Your Corporate Culture

Whether you're running a Web design business, a flower shop, or a Fortune 500 company, you need to begin today to reevaluate your corporate culture. It plays a critical factor in how your customers perceive you, how your employees feel about you, and your organization's chances to grow.

You certainly have a culture in your organization. But do you know precisely what it is? Are you leading the organization to bridge the gap between what you offer and what your customers crave through the establishment of an organizational ethos that is obsessed with enhancing relationships with your clients? Or do you merely focus—as so many companies do—on product and service? Are you as unaware of the impact of the corporate culture—and as devoid of culture—as it seems my hometown and current residence have been in the past?

My experience through Obsidian Enterprises, as well as the hundreds of organizations with which I have become familiar through my speaking and consulting work, has taught me that the disconnections between organizations and customers will be most thoroughly bridged when companies do two things:

1. Pay attention to the culture of the organization.

2. Create a "Culture of the Customer."

Let's take a look at these two points.

Pay Attention to the Culture of the Organization

Sounds so simple, doesn't it? Perhaps some reading this will be slightly offended—this is much too basic, right? Well, I certainly hope it is for you and your organization. However, too many companies will worry more about the price of their products than the congruency of their culture.

When I think about CEOs and business owners who deride the talk about an organization's culture as "soft," I'm reminded of the first

President Bush. He once mocked a reporter for asking him about "that vision thing." Yet, by ridiculing the question, he proved he didn't really have a passionate vision. When Bill Clinton presented the public with his vision—how he was going to change, if you will, the corporate culture of America—voters responded. If you want your voters (called customers) to cast their ballots (called dollars) for you and your organization, you have to understand that you express your vision to them daily through the execution of your corporate culture.

FedEx is an example of a company that has paid a great deal of attention to the importance of the culture it has established. It's difficult to think of another business that requires as much teamwork on the part of the employees as FedEx does getting your package just about anywhere in the world "absolutely, positively overnight." The important thing to note is that this is not just a catchy advertising slogan—it speaks to what FedEx is all about. In its Manager's Guide, FedEx makes this culturally telling comment: "Each link [in the chain] upholds the others and is in turn upheld by them." When that statement is made in the guidebook all managers receive, do you believe it is possible for them to feel as though managers are significantly more important than those they lead? Of course not—every person supports the others, and the others support every person. That's in the culture of FedEx.

Do you believe it is merely a coincidence that the paragons of customer commitment and loyalty are also those organizations that have built powerful and differentiated corporate cultures? When you view the list compiled by *Forbes* magazine of the "100 Best Places to Work," is it mere "luck" that every single one of them has paid a significant amount of attention to corporate culture?

I have given several speeches to the top company on the list, financial service leader Edward Jones. I've met hundreds of their people—and I have yet to meet the first dissatisfied employee. Seriously. I've never met anyone who works for Edward Jones who feels slighted, ignored, unmotivated, or disgruntled. Jones, by the way, spends 3.8 percent of its payroll on employee education—averaging 146 hours for every employee! As we discussed earlier, educating people plays a powerful role in developing customer loyalty; however, education also provides another major benefit: it prevents your organization from becoming trapped in the past. Edward Jones is hiring while most other firms in its industry are contracting. We call this . . . a *clue*!

By the way, the list of the "100 Best Places to Work" cites an unbelievable number of innovative approaches—all designed to ensure that every employee understands the organizational culture and is involved in it on a daily basis. Smucker's, for example, offers every employee at its Orrville, Ohio, home the opportunity to be a "taste tester" for its products. Pella Windows hasn't had a layoff since 1925. Baptist Health Care has a "no secrets" policy—literally meaning that a housekeeper has access to the same financial information as the CFO. A study of Qualcomm personnel found that 90 percent—yes, you read that right, *90 percent*—of those employed there say they "look forward to coming to work each day." (I dare you to take a similar study in your organization!) If you work for MBNA and are getting married, your company will pitch in five hundred bucks *and* a limo for your wedding ceremony—as well as give you an extra week off! When I spoke for the family-owned S. C. Johnson and Son (makers of consumer products such as Windex and Pledge), I found that they started their profit-sharing program in 1917—and one-third of the workforce has been there at least twenty years! Medtronic's CEO personally presents every new employee with a medallion and a copy of the corporate values.

Obviously, these highly successful organizations are spending a great deal of time focusing their attention on the culture in which their employees work, and in which they therefore create experiences for their customers. Is your organization doing anything worthy of joining this list? If not . . . when are you going to start?

Create a Culture of the Customer

The first work on corporate culture was probably done in 1939, when researchers studying Western Electric found that workers formed their own informal traditions. These unofficial institutions had tremendous impact on the success or failure of any business. Understandably, visionary organizations began to examine how they could marshal the power of the culture to enhance the viability and profitability of their company.

In his book on FedEx, *The World on Time* (Knowledge Exchange, 1996), author James C. Wetherbe cites an aborted takeover of media giant Time (later to have its own takeover woes with America Online) by Paramount. Time succeeded by "arguing that the acquisition would irreparably damage its culture. The presiding judge agreed, stating that the law could recognize any threat to a corporate culture, if the culture was shown to be palpable, distinctive, and advantageous to the conduct of business."

The culture your organization creates can enhance employee retention, improve profitability, *and*, it appears, even defend you against corporate raiders. Yet working on a culture for your organization is most effective when it centers on building relationships with customers.

In an article on corporate culture on the website of the Cupertino, California-based HR company Auxillium West (www.auxillium.com), they cite the September 1995 issue of *ACA News* and its report on studies regarding the elements of a corporate culture that fostered a team spirit within an organization. The elements noted by Auxillium West are as follows: common and consistent goals; organizational commitment; role clarity among team members; team leadership; mutual accountability with the team; complementary knowledge and skills; reinforcement of required behavioral competencies; power (real and perceived); and shared rewards.

There's no way to argue with these components. However, these building blocks of a team-oriented corporate culture will fail to have the maximum impact for an organization unless the overriding goal is simply this: *to profitably create experiences that are so compelling to customers that their loyalty becomes assured.*

Thus Completes the Circle

Which, of course, brings us full circle. Organizations must develop an ardor for customers that transcends mere product or service. When managers and executives truly display leadership, their vision of an obsession for customer loyalty will naturally encourage strategies that enhance the role of the employee. The organization's team of employees is then empowered to develop and execute approaches that build their customers' levels of trust, connection, and loyalty.

Your challenge is to build a corporate culture that is so customer obsessed that you and your employees create innovative approaches that bridge the gap and resolve the six disconnections that impair customer relationships and client loyalty.

If you accomplish that task, your company will receive one of the highest accolades in business—to be known as an organization that provides customers with what they REALLY want.

Bridge Building
Moving Toward the "Culture of the Customer"

Questions to assist you in developing your plans of action:

- How would you define and describe your organization's culture? Write your answer and pass it around to your colleagues. Is there a clear and concise view of what the company culture is?
  - Is that culture what you would desire it to be?
- How much attention are you paying to "that vision thing"? Do you understand the monumental impact it has in customer and employee loyalty?
  - If you understand it...then, describe it. Write it down.
  - Ask your colleagues to do the same. Do they "get it" as much as you do?
- What is your organization doing for new employees to assist them in understanding the corporate culture and integrating it into their daily activities?
- The final—and most important—questions:
  - *Is your organization offering what your clients crave?*
  - *Are you providing what YOUR customers REALLY want?*

NOTES

Introduction

1. Hubbie Smith, "Grocers Need to Offer Choice to Build Customer Loyalty, Industry Expert Says," *Las Vegas Review-Journal.*

2. Rohini Ahluwalia, Rao Unnava, and Robert Burnkrant, "Toward Understanding the Value of a Loyal Customer," *Marketing Science Institute newsletter,* Fall 1999.

Chapter 1

1. Timothy Keinigham, Douglas Pruden, and Terry Vavra, "Beyond Mere Satisfaction, the Role of Customer Delight," published on the Web site of consulting firm Ipsos Loyalty.

2. http://www-306.ibm.com/software/success/cssdb.nsf/CS/AKLR-5F5SCP?OpenDocument&Site=default

3. DMReview.com., March 5, 2004

4. Published on Fool.com in a series of commentaries beginning in June 2003.

5. According to an article released on Business Wire on January 22, 2003.

6. Joseph Lampel and Henry Mintzberg, "Customizing Customization," *Logistics Management & Distribution Report, Sloan Management Review,* Fall 1996.

7. As reported by Ginger Conlon in an article from *destinationCRM.com* on April 1, 2004.

8. As reported on the Web site of Empire State College, www.esc.edu.

9. From an interview with David Whitwam, the highly successful and recently retired CEO of Whirlpool, "The Right Way to Go Global," *Harvard Business Review,* March 1, 1994.

Chapter 2

1. Philippe Suchet, ClickZ.com, January 4, 2004.
2. "Lead the Field," recording (Nightengale-Conant Publishing)
3. Roger von Oech, *A Whack on the Side of the Head* (Warner Business Books, rev. ed., 1998).
4. W. Michael Cox with Richard Alm, *Consumers' Research Magazine,* June 1999.
5. Erick Schonfeld, "The Customized, Digitized, Have-it-your-way Economy," *Fortune,* September 28, 1998.
6. Joseph Lampel and Henry Mintzberg, "Logistics Management & Distribution Report: Customizing Customization," *Sloan Management Review,* Fall 1996.
7. James Gilmore and Joseph Pine, "The Four Faces of Mass Customization," *Harvard Business Review,* January 1, 1997.
8. John Graham, "How to Get Your Company Where You Want It in 2004," *The Youngstown (Ohio) Business Journal,* December 1, 2003.
9. Interview with David Whitwam, "The Right Way to Go Global," *Harvard Business Review,* March 1, 1994.

Chapter 3

1. Hunter Jameson, *Investor's Business Daily,* in articles published in August 1999.
2. Carole Nicolaides, "Focus On Soft Skills: A Leadership Wake-Up Call," published in several journals, including the Winter 2002 issue of "ASTD Quarterly" by the Smokey Mountain Chapter of the American Society for Training and Development.
3. Brian Garrity, "Online Fan Clubs Serve As Potential Profit Centers" *Billboard,* August 17, 2002.
4. Dr. LeBoeuf's book was later published as *Getting Results! The Secret to Motivating Yourself and Others* (Berkeley Publishing, June 1989).
5. John R. Ward, "Now hear this: Without listening, there is no communication," *Communication World,* July 1, 1990.
6. James Patterson and Peter Kim, *The Day America Told the Truth* (Prentice Hall Press, May, 1991).
7. M. E. Porter, "Competitive Advantage: Creating and Sustaining Superior Performance," *The Free Press,* 1985.
8. Chris Woodyard, *USA Today,* May 22, 2001.
9. *USA Today,* February 12, 2004.
10. www.LoyaltyRules.com

Chapter 4

1. Eric Schlosser, *Fast Food Nation* (Perennial Books, 2002).

2. Joshua Kennon, Web site *Investing for Beginners*, http://beginnersinvest.about.com.

3. Ellen Rohr, "Price Wars," *Entrepreneur*, April 20, 2000.

4. David Moin, "Boredom on the Runways," *Women's Wear Daily*, January 16, 1990.

5. Cited in a Gallup Press article by Ashok Gopal (of the Gallup Organization), "Managing in an Economy of Emotion, Not Reason," February 2004.

6. Greg Smith, "Employee Involvement Programs Drive Performance," www.chartcourse.com.

7. Sarah Cunningham article in the *Observer*, September 28, 2003.

8. Dr. Scott MacStravic, "Strategic differentiation becoming 'watchword' for health care organizations," *Health Care Strategic Management*, August 2000.

9. "Using Swot technique to develop objective analysis," *New Straits Times*, April 13, 2003.

10. Hedda Schupak, "Give 'em a SWOT," *Jewelers Circular Keystone*, February 2001 article.

11. Porter's argument is featured in many articles, most notably a March 2001 article by Keith Hammonds in *Fast Company* and an April 2002 piece by the Chartered Management Institute in *Thinkers* magazine.

Chapter 5

1. Merideth Levinson article on the Sears study, cited in *CIO* magazine, August 2002.

2. Dr. Sigal Barsade, "The ripple effect: emotional contagion and its influence on group behavior," *Administrative Science Quarterly*, December 2002 (At the time, Barsade was an associate professor of organizational behavior at the Yale University School of Management, and he is currently associate professor at The Wharton School at the University of Pennsylvania.)

3. "Beyond Cheap Prices—the New Era of Travel Planning." *Hotel Marketing*, January 2003.

4. Lisa Casinger, "Living the Luxe Life," *Home Accents Today*.

5. Dr. Andrea Dixon, Dr. Julie Gassenheimer and Dr. Terri Feldman Barr, "Bridging the Distance Between Us," *Journal of Personal Selling and Sales Management*, September 2002.

6. Charles M. Farkas and Suzy Wetlaufer, "The Way Chief Executive Officers Lead," *Harvard Business Review*, May 1996.

7. Julian Sparkes (managing partner of Accenture Global Travel Services Industry Group), "Enhancing the Customer Franchise," *Hotels*, December 2002.

8. Roger Trapp, "In the Digital Age, Don't Forget the Human Touch," *Independent Sunday*, June 20, 2004.

9. Caroline E. Mayer, "Customer Dis-service: These Days Customers May As Well Keep Their Complaints to Themselves," *Washington Post*, March 28, 2004.

10. Robert Hall (managing director of Xchange), "The Emphasis Reverts to Local,"*Bank Marketing*, May 2001.

11. Keith Wegner, "Toward a rhetoric of technical professionals," *Technical Communication*, February 1992.

12. Cheryl and Peter Reimhold, "Giving technical presentations for non-technical audiences," *Solutions*, December 2003.

Chapter 6

1. Dan Debicella, "Innovation and Imitation—Positional Determinants of Success and Failure," Wharton School Web site, www.wharton.upenn.edu.

2. Dr. Behna N. Tabrizi and Dr. Kathleen Eisenhardt, "Accelerating adaptive processes: product innovation in the global computer industry," *Administrative Science Quarterly*, March 1995.

3. Ron Jonash, "Product Innovation: Staying Ahead of the Competition," *USA Today Sunday*, January 2000.

4. "The Long Road to Success," *American Machinist*, September 2003.

5. Diane Brady, "Why Service Stinks," *Business Week*, October 23, 2003.

6. Steven Gray, "Crossing Blades for Face Time," *Washington Post*, January 2, 2004.

7. Michael J. Weiss, "To Be About to Be," *American Demographics*, September 2003.

8. Gary Hamel, "Innovation Now! (It's the Only Way to Survive)," *Fast Company*, December 2002.

9. Sian Harrington, "Sharper NPD at Heinz," *Grocer*, June 23, 2003.

10. Stephanie Stahl, "Business Execs Get Lessons in Leadership," *Information Week*, May 10, 2004.

ABOUT THE AUTHOR

Scott McKain is Vice Chairman of Obsidian Enterprises, recently named one of the "fastest growing public companies" in the country—as well as Vice Chairman of Durham Capital Corporation. In addition, McKain is the cofounder of The Value Added Institute, a think-tank researching the impact on organizations of creating the enhanced customer experiences that generate greater client loyalty. His client list for speeches, seminars and consulting is a "Who's Who" of corporations (such as GE, IBM, General Dynamics, Philips, and literally hundreds more) as well as state and national associations representing a highly diverse range of industries and interests. He has appeared on platforms in all fifty states and fourteen countries.

A member of the Professional Speakers Hall of Fame, Scott also makes appearances on FOX News Channel and other major media outlets as an expert commentator. Scott, his wife Tammy, and sons Corbin and Faron Byler live in Indianapolis, Indiana.

If you would like more information on Scott McKain's speeches and seminars, consulting services, video and audio programs, and other projects of assistance to organizations seeking to discover "what customers REALLY want" and to execute strategies to bridge the gaps of customer disconnections, contact your favorite speakers bureau or:

Modern Management
1625 Broadway; Sixth Floor
Nashville TN 37203

Phone: 615-742-0099
Fax: 615-742-0088

Or visit our Web sites:

www.ScottMcKain.com
www.ValueAddedInstitute.com

www.ObsidianEnterprises.com
www.ModMgmt.com

ACKNOWLEDGMENTS

This book—just as my first, *ALL Business Is Show Business*—would not have happened without the extraordinary belief and dedication of Ted Greene, founding partner of Modern Management. I am extremely grateful to all the staff of Modern Management for their hard work on my behalf.

I dedicated my first book to my best friend, Tim Durham, Chairman and CEO of Obsidian Enterprises—and I am eternally thankful for his friendship. It is my honor to serve as vice chairman of our organization—and a special thanks to all of our employees, who work every day to provide our customers with what they REALLY want.

This project became reality thanks to Brian Hampton of Nelson Business. My appreciation, as well, to Kyle Olund and Kristen Lucas for their efforts. This is my second book with the Nelson team—and they provide me with an "ultimate author experience."

As always, thanks to Shelley Erwin of Performance Marketing Group and McKainErwin Company for my outstanding Web site—and for being my favorite sister! It truly is all about you!

My partner in The Value Added Institute, Bruce Johnston, is a great colleague, friend, and adviser. I'm grateful to him, as well as his wonderful wife, Dawna.

ACKNOWLEDGMENTS

My literary agent, Mel Berger of the William Morris Agency, is a tremendous inspiration to me. He is one of the true legends in the publishing business—yet somehow finds the time to represent this little business writer.

No one could have better professional colleagues than I possess with my fellow members of Speakers Roundtable. Their generosity is amazing—and their friendship beyond description. It is such an honor to be a part of this group.

Thanks, as well, to the speakers' bureaus and clients across the country, who keep my calendar full.

Heartfelt appreciation to the best buddies a guy could have—my pals in the greatest band in the history of country music, Diamond Rio. My first book was also dedicated to Brian Prout—and I would be remiss if I didn't thank Dana Williams for his dedication and concern for my family during very difficult times. Thanks to Gene Johnson, Jimmy Olander, Dan Truman, and Marty Roe. You guys rock! (But not too much—you're a country band!)

My appreciation, as well, to the many authors and speakers who have given me ideas and assisted in the development of both the idea behind this book and the manuscript.

Finally—and most important—thanks to YOU for taking the time to read this book. I sincerely hope it will be of value to you.

Every day your organization—and you—are in the spotlight. Your employees are performing and the audience—your customers—will love the show, hate it, or worst of all ignore it. Scott McKain has discovered what the film, television, and music industries have known for years: to be successful, you must create an emotional link with your audience.

- Tell your story well. It will make you a star.
- Have a short, powerful, and unique high concept statement. It worked for Jaws and it will work for you.
- Practice the eight essential acts your customers want you to perform.
- Your employees are the stars of the show. Treat them that way.
- Create the Ultimate Customer Experience, and you will acquire amazing loyalty and unlimited referrals.

"No matter what your business," says Scott McKain, "you are always on stage. Make your performance one that leaves your customers with a feeling of Wow!"

". . . preparatory to going to work in the morning, every retailer and service person should be compelled to read Scott McKain's wonderful book, "ALL Business is Show Business." The Premier and the Mayor should demand that everyone in tourism, service and retail read this book. It's all about amazing and thrilling your customers and making them loyal for life. It's about providing unforgettable . . . experiences and making emotional connections that remain long after the party's over."

David Berner
Columnist, Vancouver Lifestyles Magazine
Talk Show Host; CKNW Radio; Vancouver, BC

Printed in the United States
123231LV00003B/2/A

9 780785 288367